THEVEGETARIANBIBLE

MARKS &
SPENCER

THEVEGETARIANBIBLE

consultant editor
NICOLA GRAIMES

Marks and Spencer p.l.c.
P.O. Box 3339
Chester CH99 9QS
www.marksandspencer.com

ISBN: 1-84461-324-0

Printed in China

Created and produced by The Bridgewater Book Company Ltd
Project editor: Sarah Doughty
Project designer: Anna Hunter-Downing
Commissioned photography: Clive Bozzard-Hill

Notes for the reader

This book uses both metric and imperial measurements. Follow the
same units of measurement throughout; do not mix metric and
imperial. All spoon measurements are level: teaspoons are assumed to
be 5 ml, and tablespoons are assumed to be 15 ml. Unless otherwise
stated, milk is assumed to be full fat, eggs and individual vegetables
such as potatoes are medium and pepper is freshly ground black
pepper. Recipes using raw or very lightly cooked eggs should be
avoided by infants, the elderly, pregnant women, convalescents and
anyone suffering from an illness. The times given are an approximate
guide only. Preparation times differ according to the techniques used
by different people and the cooking times may also vary from those
given. Optional ingredients, variations or serving suggestions have not
been included in the calculations.

Picture acknowledgements

The Bridgewater Book Company would like to thank the following
for permission to reproduce copyright material:
Corbis pp. 11, 45, 168 and front cover.

CONTENTS

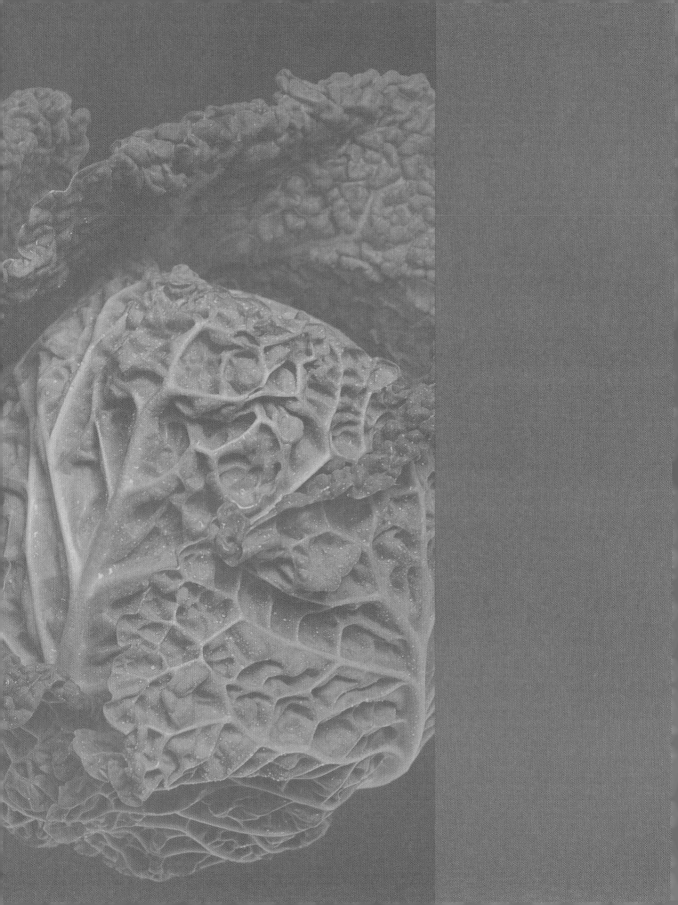

1

The Vegetarian Bible is a comprehensive reference book that will help you prepare and enjoy healthy vegetarian meals. Whether you are new to vegetarianism, looking for renewed inspiration or you simply want to cut down the amount of meat in your diet, you will find lots of new ideas for recipes and ways of cooking vegetarian meals.

INTRODUCTION

Vegetables are, of course, at the heart of a vegetarian diet. There is a huge variety of delicious vegetables to choose from, all full of goodness and nutrients. Eating a balanced diet, which also includes fruit, eggs, dairy, nuts, seeds, lentils and pulses, is very important and can be achieved by careful planning and combining of foods. The recipes in this book will whet your appetite for healthy vegetarian living, and provide dishes that are ideal for every occasion.

What is a Vegetarian?

A vegetarian is someone who chooses not to eat meat, poultry, fish or by-products of meat and fish, such as gelatine. Lacto ovo vegetarians include eggs and dairy products in their diet, while lacto vegetarians avoid eggs. Vegetarians who avoid dairy products and eggs, and non-food items produced from animals are known as vegans.

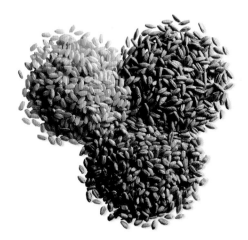

WHY BE VEGETARIAN?

There are many reasons for becoming vegetarian. Some people give up meat and fish because they morally do not approve of killing animals, or because they are unhappy with ways in which animals are kept or killed for food. Some are concerned about the effect that keeping livestock for meat is having on land that could otherwise be used for growing crops, as well as for environmental reasons. Many people are also becoming vegetarian because of the health benefits it can offer them.

WHAT ARE THE BENEFITS?

Vegetables, fruit, nuts, seeds, lentils, pulses, eggs and dairy products provide a wide range of nutrients that can boost the immune system and improve general health. Numerous research studies show that those who choose to go vegetarian are likely to boost their health and longevity. For instance, vegetarians experience 30 per cent less heart disease, up to 40 per cent less cancer and 20 per cent less premature mortality. In addition, those with a healthy vegetarian diet usually have lower blood pressure and reduced occurrence of diet-related diabetes and obesity.

WHAT ARE THE PITFALLS?

As with any diet, balance is the key to good health. Like everyone else, vegetarians need to eat a range of foods. Simply replacing the meat part of a meal with a plate of vegetables or a slab of high-fat cheese will not provide all the nutrients required by the body. A vegetarian diet can provide all the nutrients you need and it often contains higher amounts of the antioxidant vitamins C, E and beta carotene. However, it is advisable to make sure that you also get adequate amounts of iron, zinc and B vitamins, especially B12. Although it is only required in small amounts, vitamin B12 is essential for maintaining the nervous system. Good sources of B12 for vegetarians are cheese and eggs, and fortified foods such as yeast extract, breakfast cereals, soya milk, sunflower margarine and textured vegetable protein.

The mineral zinc is essential for a healthy immune system and skin, and can be found in dairy products, beans, lentils, nuts, seeds (particularly pumpkin), wholegrains and yeast-based foods. A vegetarian diet often contains less zinc than a meat-based one, so it is important to supplement your diet with foods that provide this mineral. Iron deficiency is one of the most prevalent nutritional problems for vegetarians and non-vegetarians alike. Iron is essential for the formation of haemoglobin, the red pigment in blood. Iron from animal sources is more readily absorbed than that found in plant sources, so it is important for vegetarians to make sure that they eat adequate amounts. Good sources include beans, lentils, wholegrains, eggs, leafy green vegetables, black treacle, dairy products, fortified breakfast cereals, brown rice, broccoli and dried fruit. Vitamin C aids the absorption of iron – a glass of orange juice with a meal is a simple way of boosting your daily vitamin C intake.

above left *Grains are an important source of energy in a diet.*

below *At least two portions of fruit should be eaten every day.*

right *A healthy diet includes a balance of different foods.*

The Foods We Need

A well-balanced vegetarian diet provides all the nutrients you need for good health. It is important to achieve a good balance of nutrients – protein, carbohydrate, vitamins, minerals and some fat. Vegetarians need to be sure that they eat a variety of protein foods such as eggs, nuts, lentils, tofu, pulses and dairy products. Combining these with starchy foods such as potatoes, wholegrains, rice or pasta on a daily basis will ensure that you achieve the desired range of nutrients.

CEREALS, GRAINS AND POTATOES

This diverse group of foods, also known as complex carbohydrates, includes oats, wheat, corn, millet, barley, rye and rice, along with their derivatives such as bread and pasta. Grains have been the staple food of many civilizations for thousands of years: wheat, barley, oats and rye in Europe; maize in America, quinoa in South America, rice in the Far East and millet in Africa. Despite the current popularity of low-carb diets, this group of foods is our main and most important source of energy. However, there are good and bad carbohydrates: the best are the unrefined types such as wholemeal bread and pasta, brown rice and potatoes with their skins on, which provide fibre, B vitamins and a range of minerals, as well as plenty of sustained energy. The carbohydrates you should cut back on, or indeed avoid, are the refined sugars found in cakes, biscuits and sugary breakfast cereals, which lead to rising and falling blood sugar levels.

DAIRY AND NON-DAIRY ALTERNATIVES

Cheese, milk and yogurt are what are known as 'first-class' protein foods because they contain all eight essential amino acids, required for maintenance and repair in the body. Yet, bear in mind that many dairy products, particularly cheese, cream and butter, are also high in saturated fat. Low-fat cheese (mozzarella, feta, ricotta and reduced-fat Cheddar, etc.), yogurt and milk are just as good, providing calcium, vitamin A, B12 and D. If you choose to avoid dairy products, there are now plenty of alternatives made from soya, nuts and oats, which are often fortified with vitamins and minerals. Eggs are also included in this group; a maximum of 3–4 is recommended a week.

FRUIT AND VEGETABLES

Fruit and vegetables should form a major part of everyone's diet, because they are a good source of vitamins, minerals and fibre and are low in fat and calories. Dried fruit is a good source of fibre and iron, but contains negligible amounts of vitamin C.

Recent research has identified a number of natural plant compounds that may play a crucial role in preventing cancer, heart disease, arthritis and diabetes, along with many other health problems. These compounds are collectively known as phytochemicals and are also found in other plant foods such as wholegrains, pulses, nuts and seeds. To benefit fully from the range of phytochemicals, you should eat at least five different types of fruit and vegetables a day. Cruciferous vegetables such as broccoli, cabbage, Brussels sprouts, chard and cauliflower provide a beneficial combination of antioxidants, which support the immune system, protecting it against potentially

left *Proteins from dairy foods such as milk or yogurt provide essential amino acids.*

above left *Potatoes in their skins are a healthy option, providing fibre.*

harmful free radicals in the body. Orange, red and yellow fresh produce are rich in the antioxidant beta carotene and vitamin C.

It is vital to buy fruit and vegetables as fresh as possible to benefit from their range of nutrients. Buy organic, seasonal and locally grown produce, if possible, and avoid wilted and bruised specimens; not only will they taste inferior, but their nutrients will have diminished.

above *The main nutrients in fruit are to be found just below the skin. It is healthiest to eat them raw.*

right *It is easy to boost your fibre intake with high-fibre cereals for breakfast.*

HOW MUCH FIBRE?

Few people get enough fibre. On average, we eat about 12 g/½ oz of fibre a day, but the recommended amount is around 18–20 g/⅔–¾ oz. Fruit, vegetables, wholegrains, pulses and nuts are our main source of insoluble and soluble fibre. The former helps to combat constipation, while soluble fibre can help to reduce blood cholesterol and control blood sugar levels.

The following are some simple ways to boost your fibre intake:

- Base your diet on wholemeal bread, pasta and rice with plentiful amounts of fruit and vegetables. If feasible, avoid peeling fruit and vegetables, since the skins contain valuable fibre.
- Porridge, wholegrain cereals and muesli are the perfect high-fibre way to start the day.
- Dried fruit is rich in fibre: add it to stews, cereals, yogurt, pies, cakes and puddings – either chopped or puréed.
- Add beans and lentils to soups, stews, bakes and pies to boost their fibre content.

PULSES

Dried peas, beans and lentils are known as pulses and form a valuable part of a vegetarian diet, since they contain a higher proportion of protein than most other plant foods. They are also an important source of B vitamins, iron, calcium, zinc and fibre, as well as being low in fat. Do not feel you have to spend hours soaking dried pulses; there is much to be said for canned ones: they taste good, are incredibly convenient and dispense with lengthy cooking and soaking times. Additionally, canned pulses retain about half their

vitamin C content after processing, yet this diminishes almost completely when dried. If you choose to soak and boil your own, cook double the quantity required and freeze for later use.

The soya bean is nutritionally superior to other types of pulse, since it is a complete protein (contains all eight essential amino acids) and is higher in iron and calcium. Tofu, tempeh, miso, soya milk, yogurt and soya mince can all make invaluable, nutritious additions to a meat-free diet.

Lentils come in various types and are versatile, nutritious and easy to cook. Try adding to soups, stews and bakes to boost their protein content.

NUTS AND SEEDS

A good source of B vitamins, iron, magnesium, calcium, vitamin E, selenium, potassium, zinc and omega-6 essential fatty acids, nuts and seeds also provide valuable protein. Peanuts and coconuts, though, are high in saturated fat, so eat in moderation. Opt for unsalted nuts; not only do they make a nutritious snack, but also give a healthy boost to pies, stews, desserts

left *Pulses are a valuable and versatile source of protein in a vegetarian diet.*

below *Red lentils, being split, are quicker to cook from dried than other types.*

and cakes. In Chinese medicine, walnuts are known as the 'longevity fruit' and are one of the few plant foods that provide both omega-3 and omega-6 essential fatty acids (EFAs). Pumpkin seeds also include both types of EFAs, while Brazil nuts and sunflower and sesame seeds and their oils are particularly rich in omega-6 fatty acids. Buy them as fresh as possible, preferably in their shells, since they can become rancid if stored for too long, and keep in an airtight container, away from the light.

WARNING
Nuts can be the cause of a severe allergy with life-threatening symptoms. If there is any history of nut allergy within your family, consult your doctor before giving nuts to your child. Children under five should not be given whole nuts due to the risk of choking.

above *Nuts have plenty of nutrients, but contain high levels of saturated fats.*

left *Fats and oils are essential for the body in moderate amounts.*

FATS AND OILS

We all know that too much fat is bad for us, but a moderate amount of the appropriate type is essential for a healthy brain and eyes, keeping tissues in good repair, for the production of hormones and to transport some vitamins around the body. A high intake of saturated fat is linked to raised cholesterol levels and heart disease, whereas unsaturated (mono- and polyunsaturated) fat can help to reduce harmful cholesterol levels in the body. Polyunsaturated fats provide the much talked about essential fatty acids omega-3 and omega-6. Fish oils are the richest source of omega-3 fatty acids. Although omega-3 is not so widely available in a vegetarian diet, you need not miss out: linseeds and flaxseed oil, rapeseed oil, walnuts, eggs, pumpkin seeds and tofu provide varying amounts. It may also be worth considering taking a suitable supplement. Omega-6 is provided by plant oils, nuts and seeds, while olive oil is a monounsaturated fat.

WHAT YOU SHOULD EAT EVERY DAY...

- 5 or more servings of fruit and vegetables
- 3–4 servings of cereals/grains or potatoes
- 2–3 servings of pulses, nuts and seeds
- 2 servings of milk, cheese, eggs or soya products
- A small amount of fat/oils, such as olive, sunflower, butter or unhydrogenated margarine

Source: The Vegetarian Society

Essential Vitamins and Minerals

VITAMIN/MINERAL	FUNCTION	GOOD VEGETARIAN SOURCES	PROBLEMS CAUSED BY DEFICIENCY
VITAMIN A (retinol in animal foods, beta carotene in plant foods)	For healthy vision, bone growth, skin and tissue repair. Beta carotene acts as an antioxidant and supports the immune system	Dairy products, egg yolk, margarine, carrots, apricots, squash, red peppers, broccoli, green leafy vegetables, mango, dried apricots and sweet potatoes	Poor night vision, dry skin and impaired immune system, especially respiratory disorders
VITAMIN B1 (thiamine)	Essential for breaking down carbohydrates for energy as well as the nervous system, muscles and heart, promotes growth and boosts mental well-being	Wholegrain cereals, brewer's yeast, yeast extract, Brazil nuts, sunflower seeds, peanuts, rice, bran and mycoprotein (Quorn®)	Depression, irritability, nervous disorders, memory loss. Common among alcoholics
VITAMIN B2 (riboflavin)	Essential for energy production as well as healthy skin, tissue repair and maintenance	Cheese, eggs, milk, yogurt, fortified breakfast cereals, yeast extract, almonds, wholemeal bread, mushrooms, prunes, cashew nuts and pumpkin seeds	Lack of energy, skin problems, dry cracked lips, numbness and itchy eyes
VITAMIN B3 (niacin)	Essential for energy production, healthy digestive system, skin and nervous system	Pulses, yeast extract, potatoes, fortified breakfast cereals, wheatgerm, peanuts, cheese, eggs, mushrooms, green leafy vegetables, figs, prunes and sesame seeds	Deficiency is unusual, but characterized by lack of energy, depression and scaly skin
VITAMIN B6 (pyridoxine)	Essential for assimilating protein and fat, red blood cell formation and a healthy immune system	Eggs, wheatgerm, wholemeal flour, yeast extract, breakfast cereals, peanuts, bananas, currants and lentils	Anaemia, dermatitis and depression
VITAMIN B12 (cyanocobalamin)	Essential for red blood cell formation, growth, healthy nervous system and energy formation	Dairy products, eggs, fortified breakfast cereals, cheese, yeast extract, fortified soya milk	Fatigue, poor resistance to infection, breathlessness and anaemia
Folate (folic acid)	Essential for red blood cell formation, making genetic material (DNA) and protein synthesis. Extra is needed pre-conception and during pregnancy to protect foetus against neural tube defects	Green leafy vegetables, broccoli, fortified breakfast cereals, bread, nuts, pulses, bananas, yeast extract and asparagus	Anaemia, appetite loss and linked to neural defects in babies
VITAMIN C (ascorbic acid)	Essential for healthy skin, teeth, bones, gums, immune system, resistance to infection, energy production and growth	Citrus fruit, melons, strawberries, tomatoes, broccoli, potatoes, peppers and green leafy vegetables	Impaired immune system, fatigue, insomnia and depression
VITAMIN D	Essential for healthy teeth and bones, aids absorption of calcium and phosphate	Sunlight, non-hydrogenated vegetable margarine, vegetable oils, eggs and dairy products	Bone and muscle weakness. Long-term shortage results in rickets

VITAMIN/MINERAL	FUNCTION	GOOD VEGETARIAN SOURCES	PROBLEMS CAUSED BY DEFICIENCY
VITAMIN E (tocopherol)	Essential for healthy skin, circulation and maintaining cells. As an antioxidant, it protects vitamins A and C in the body	Seeds, wheatgerm, nuts, vegetable oils, eggs, wholemeal bread, green leafy vegetables, oats, sunflower oil, avocado and fortified breakfast cereals	Increased risk of heart disease, strokes and certain cancers
VITAMIN K	Essential for effective blood clotting	Spinach, cabbage and cauliflower	Deficiency is rare
Calcium	Essential for building and maintaining bones and teeth, muscle function and the nervous system	Dairy products, green leafy vegetables, sesame seeds, broccoli, dried fruit, pulses, almonds, spinach, watercress and tofu	Soft and brittle bones, osteoporosis, fractures and muscle weakness
Iron	Essential component of haemoglobin, which transports oxygen in the blood	Egg yolk, fortified breakfast cereals, green leafy vegetables, dried fruit, cashew nuts, pulses, wholegrains, tofu, pumpkin seeds, black treacle and brown rice	Anaemia, fatigue and low resistance to infection
Magnesium	Essential for healthy muscles, bones and teeth, normal growth and energy production	Nuts, seeds, wholegrains, pulses, tofu, dried figs, dried apricots and green vegetables	Deficiency rare, but characterized by lethargy, weak bones and muscles, depression and irritability
Phosphorus	Essential for healthy bones and teeth, muscle function, energy production and the assimilation of nutrients, particularly calcium	Found in most foods: milk, cheese, yogurt, eggs, nuts, seeds, pulses and wholegrains	Deficiency is rare
Potassium	Important in maintaining the body's water balance, normal blood pressure and nerve transmission	Bananas, milk, pulses, nuts, seeds, wholegrains, potatoes, fruit and root vegetables	Weakness, thirst, fatigue, mental confusion and raised blood pressure
Selenium	Essential for protecting against free radical damage and for red blood cell function as well as healthy hair and skin	Avocado, lentils, milk, cheese, wholemeal bread, cashew nuts, walnuts, seaweed and sunflower seeds	Reduced immunity
Zinc	Essential for a healthy immune system, tissue formation, normal growth, wound healing and reproduction	Peanuts, cheese, wholegrains, sunflower and pumpkin seeds, pulses, milk, hard cheese, yogurt, wheatgerm and mycoprotein (Quorn®)	Impaired growth and development, slow wound healing and loss of taste and smell

Planning Meals

The key to a good diet is variety. A balanced meal combines sufficient amounts of protein, carbohydrate, fibre, the right types of fat, vitamins and minerals. The ideal diet includes enough calories to provide the body with vital energy, but not an excess, which leads to weight gain.

above *Stir-frying is a quick and nutritious way to cook.*

KEEPING A MEAL BALANCED

Make sure each meal contains a protein (eggs, pulses, tofu, dairy products, nuts and seeds) and a carbohydrate (pasta, rice, wholegrains, bread) element. Despite the current popularity of low-carb diets, it is recommended that at least 50 per cent of a meal is carbohydrate based. Remember that many foods, such as pulses and wholegrains, are a combination of protein and carbohydrate. A moderate amount of fat in the diet is essential, not only for health, but also as it contributes to the taste, texture and palatability of food. Restrict fat levels to no more than 30 per cent of your daily diet and stick to polyunsaturated fats.

VEGETARIAN CHILDREN

There is no reason why children should not thrive on a vegetarian diet – as long as it is not based on cheese sandwiches, beans and chips. However, they do have slightly different dietary requirements from adults. Young children can find fibre difficult to digest in large amounts; too much can make a child feel full before they have been able to ingest enough nutrients and can lead to stomach upset. Fibre can also interfere with the absorption of iron, zinc and calcium. Refined bran should not be added to a young child's diet.

Reduced-fat foods, such as skimmed milk and low-fat cheese, lack the much-needed calories and therefore energy required by young growing children: reduced-fat dairy products are suitable for children over two years, but younger children require the full-fat equivalent.

Parents are also advised to give their children at least five portions of fruit and vegetables a day, but unlike adults, this should be divided as three portions of fruit and two of vegetables – fruit provides plenty of energy.

Babies and young children do not have the capacity to eat large amounts and so need to eat three small nutritious meals a day, plus two healthy snacks.

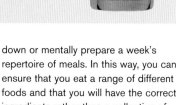

Try to include at least two different types of cooked vegetables (steamed, stir-fried, microwaved or roasted, rather than boiled) in the main meal. Or, prepare a large salad that combines a range of different types of different-coloured vegetables such as rocket, watercress, spinach, beetroot, avocado, tomatoes and carrot. Fruit or fruit-based desserts make a perfect, convenient end to a meal or low-fat snack.

Try not to stick to the same meals every week. Experiment with different foods and try out new recipes. Before you do your weekly shop, either write

down or mentally prepare a week's repertoire of meals. In this way, you can ensure that you eat a range of different foods and that you will have the correct ingredients rather than a collection of foods that do not work together.

It is a common misconception that vegetarians have to meticulously combine protein foods in every meal to achieve the correct balance of amino acids. The latest expert advice states that, provided you eat a varied range of vegetarian protein foods on a daily basis, this is sufficient; intentionally combining proteins is unnecessary.

WATCH OUT FOR...

It is always wise to check food and drink labels when shopping. The following checklist makes a useful reference guide.

ADDITIVES
These include emulsifiers, colourings and flavourings, and may or may not be vegetarian. Two of the most common are E441 (gelatine), a gelling agent derived from animal parts and bones, and E120 (cochineal), made from crushed insects.

ALBUMEN
Albumen may be derived from battery-farmed eggs.

ALCOHOL
Alcohol is clarified using animal ingredients. All cask-conditioned 'real' ales, some bottled, canned and keg bitters, milds and stouts are fined (clarified) with isinglass derived from the swim bladders of certain tropical fish. Wine may also be fined with isinglass, dried blood, egg albumen derived from battery hens, gelatine and chitin from crab and shrimp shells. Vegetarian alternatives include bentonite, kieselguhr, kaolin and silica gel. Non-vintage port is fined with gelatine.

ANIMAL FATS
Animal fats are sometimes found in biscuits, cakes, pastry, stock, chips, margarine, ready-meals, margarine and ice cream. Edible fats can mean animal fats.

ASPIC
Aspic is a savoury jelly derived from meat or fish.

CHEESE
Many cheeses are produced using animal rennet, an enzyme taken from the stomach of a calf. Vegetarian cheese is made using microbial or fungal enzymes. Non-vegetarian cheese is often used in pesto, sauces and ready-meals.

EGGS
Eggs are animal products. Some foods, such as mayonnaise or pasta, may contain battery-farmed eggs. If possible, try to buy organic, free-range eggs.

GRAVY
Gravy is made from meat juices, although vegetarian gravy mixes do exist.

JELLY
Jelly usually contains animal-derived gelatine, but it is possible to buy vegetarian alternatives set with agar agar or guar gum.

MARGARINE
Margarine may contain animal-derived vitamin D3, fats, gelatine and E numbers as well as whey.

SOFT DRINKS
Soft drinks, particularly canned orange drinks, may contain gelatine, which is used as a carrier for added beta carotene.

SOUP
Soup may contain animal stock or fat.

SUET
Suet is animal fat, but vegetarian versions do exist.

SWEETS
Sweets may contain gelatine, cochineal and animal fats.

WORCESTERSHIRE SAUCE
Most brands contain anchovies, but vegetarian versions do exist.

YOGURT, CREME FRAICHE, FROMAGE FRAIS AND ICE CREAM
Some low-fat varieties may contain gelatine.

Source: The Vegetarian Society

below *Vegetarian cheeses are readily available in shops and supermarkets.*

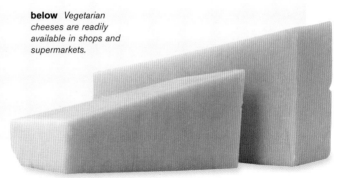

The Vegetarian Kitchen

If you have a well-stocked storecupboard, refrigerator and freezer, then creating healthy, nutritious vegetarian meals is very much easier. What is equally essential is buying good-quality ingredients, then storing, preparing and cooking them in a way that preserves as many nutrients as possible.

THE STORECUPBOARD

This list of ingredients creates a well-stocked storecupboard. It is by no means exhaustive, or you may feel that not all the foods are to your liking, but it gives a general guide to the foods to choose from.

• Canned pulses and vegetables: cannellini, flageolet, chickpeas, borlotti, kidney, butter beans, baked beans, lentils, tomatoes, sweetcorn, ratatouille, artichokes, olives and asparagus.

• Jars of sauces: black bean sauce, teriyaki sauce, hoisin, pesto, passata and satay sauce.

• Jars and tubes of flavourings: harissa (chilli paste), tomato purée, sun-dried tomato paste, soy sauce, tamari, vegetarian Worcestershire sauce, olive paste, sweet chilli sauce, miso, mustards and mayonnaise.

• Stock-based flavourings: vegetable bouillon, miso sachets, cubes.

• Flours: plain, self-raising wholemeal, white, buckwheat, gluten-free, polenta and cornflour.

• Dried pulses and lentils: chickpeas, kidney, aduki, cannellini, etc., textured vegetable protein, soya chunks or mince, as well as Puy, red and yellow lentils.

• Dried fruit: apricots, figs, prunes, dates, apples and raisins.

• Nuts and seeds: nut butters, walnuts, Brazils, cashew nuts, chopped mixed nuts, ground and sliced almonds, sunflower, pumpkin and sesame seeds.

• Grains: pasta in various shapes, rice in various types, buckwheat and egg noodles, couscous, bulgar wheat, quinoa, brown, risotto, Spanish paella, basmati and pudding rice, barley, millet and polenta.

• Oils and vinegars: olive (extra virgin and virgin), sunflower, nut, vegetable and sesame oils, white and red wine vinegar and cider, balsamic and sherry wine vinegars.

above left *Pasta, rice and cereals form an essential part of any storecupboard.*

above *Dried fruit keeps best for periods of time if the packet is well sealed.*

left *Oils and vinegars are best stored in a cool, dark place to prevent oxidation.*

• Dried herbs and spices: oregano, mixed, thyme, tarragon, saffron, coriander, cumin, chilli, cardamom, cinnamon, nutmeg, cayenne, paprika and ginger.
• Preserves and sweeteners: maple syrup, black treacle, honey, fructose (natural sugar), demerara, unrefined caster and icing sugar, high-fruit jams and curds and marmalade.
• Baked goods: wholewheat crackers, oatcakes, rice cakes, corncakes and breadsticks.

SHOPPING TIPS

Buy fresh foods from shops with a high turnover of goods, since fruit and vegetables that have been hanging around for a while are likely to be lower in vitamins and minerals. Avoid fruit and vegetables displayed in a hot, light window, since this will influence nutrient levels. Loose fresh produce is much easier to check for quality.

When buying eggs, look for organic and free-range; not only are the hens kept in preferable living conditions, they are also fed a natural diet and are not routinely fed antibiotics or yolk-enhancing dyes.

When buying packaged foods, check the labels. Avoid those with high amounts of sugar, salt, saturated and hydrogenated (trans) fat, colourings, additives, flavourings, preservatives and artificial sweeteners, many of which have been linked to food allergies, are unhealthy and are often not vegetarian.

Keep dry ingredients, including beans, grains, nuts and seeds, in small quantities and store in airtight containers in a cool, dark cupboard. If kept for too long, they can become rancid. Buy oils preferably in dark bottles and store in a cool, dark place to prevent oxidation.

GET COOKING

The way you cook and prepare food influences its nutritional content. Generally speaking, raw fruit and vegetables are richer in nutrients than cooked, but avoid peeling them, if possible, since many nutrients are found in or just below the skin. Wash or scrub vegetables, but do not soak them, as water-soluble nutrients will leach into the water. When preparing fruit and vegetables, do so just before cooking or serving, as nutrients such as vitamin C diminish as soon as the cut surface is exposed to air. Steam or stir-fry foods rather than boil them – the latter destroys water-soluble vitamins such as B and C. The cooking water can also be used as stock for soup or sauces.

above left *Keeping a supply of nutritious biscuits is a good idea.*

above *Buying loose produce helps keep a check on quality.*

GO ORGANIC

You may have to pay slightly more for organic produce, but the benefits are numerous. Organic fruit and vegetables tend to taste better because they are not intensively grown to absorb excessive water. They are generally cultivated in better-quality soil and left to ripen longer on the plant, rather than being artificially ripened, which can affect flavour and nutrient levels. Furthermore, some studies have shown that the lower levels of water in organic produce mean there is a higher concentration of vitamins and minerals. Children are believed to be more vulnerable to the effects of pesticide residues than adults.

Vegetables

Vegetables are an essential component of a healthy diet and have numerous nutritional benefits. It is recommended that we eat three different types of vegetable a day and there is no shortage of varieties to choose from. Vegetables offer the vegetarian cook an infinite number of culinary possibilities.

BRASSICAS
This large and varied group of vegetables boasts an extraordinary range of health properties and should form a regular part of our diet – at least 3–4 times a week. They provide numerous phytochemicals, a group of compounds that have been found to provide an anti-carcinogenic cocktail and play a crucial role in fighting disease by stimulating the body's defences. Brassicas are best cooked lightly. Overcooking them not only destroys many of the nutrients, but also affects their flavour. Steaming or stir-frying are preferable to boiling for this reason. Some people dislike brassicas due to their slight bitterness, yet serving them in a cream or cheese sauce may help. They also work well in Asian dishes.

CABBAGE
When lightly cooked or served shredded in a salad, cabbage is delicious. Cabbages range from the crinkly leaved Savoy, which is ideal for stuffing, to the smooth and firm white and red. Add a little vinegar to the cooking water when preparing red cabbage to preserve its colour. Chinese cabbage has a more delicate flavour and is good in salads or stir-fries.

BROCCOLI
There are two types of broccoli: the slender-stemmed purple sprouting type is the original type of broccoli, with long stalks and small purple flower heads. The leaves, stalks and head are all edible. The readily available calabrese has tightly budded top and thick stalk. Choose broccoli with dark green or purple florets and avoid any with signs of yellowing or a wilted stalk. When serving broccoli, do not forget the stalk, which is also nutritious. The stalk can be served raw; grated into salads or cut into crudités.

CAULIFLOWER
Cauliflower comes in many varieties, ranging from white to pale green and purple, but all should be encased in green outer leaves, as these protect the more delicate florets.

BRUSSELS SPROUTS

Reminiscent of Christmas, Brussels sprouts are like miniature cabbages and have a strong, nutty flavour. Sprouts are sweeter when picked after the first frost. They are best cooked very lightly or, better still, stir-fried.

LEAFY GREENS

Research into the health benefits of leafy greens shows that by eating spinach, chard, pak choi, spring greens and spinach beet on a regular basis, you may protect yourself against certain forms of cancer. Leafy vegetables are tastiest served steamed or stir-fried and go particularly well with Asian dishes that include garlic, ginger, chilli and soy sauce.

SHOOT VEGETABLES

This diverse group includes asparagus, fennel, chicory, celery and the globe artichoke. The distinguished globe artichoke has an exquisite flavour and is great fun to eat: simply boil in water, then dip each leaf into garlic butter or mayonnaise, or a vinaigrette dressing. The tastiest part is the heart, which is to be found in the centre of the vegetable, beneath the hairy choke.

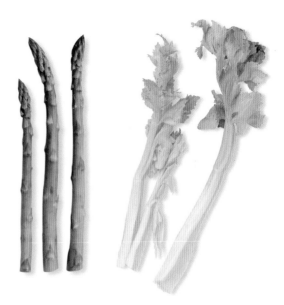

SPINACH

Spinach does provide iron, but not in such rich amounts as was once thought and in a form that is not easy to assimilate. However, combining spinach with vitamin C-rich foods increases absorption. Nutritionally, it is most beneficial when eaten raw and the young leaves are best for this.

CHARD

Like spinach, chard should have dark green leaves and a white or red stem. As the stem takes longer to cook than the leaves, it is best sliced and cooked slightly before the leaves. Spinach beet is similar to Swiss chard and has a mild flavour. Spring greens are full of flavour and nutrients and should have dark green leaves.

PAK CHOI

The most typical pak choi features dark green leaves at the top of thick, white, upright stalks. It has a mild flavour, which makes it popular with children, and makes a delightful addition to stir-fries, soups, noodle dishes and salads. The stalk takes slightly longer to cook than the leaves.

ASPARAGUS

There are two types of asparagus: white is picked just before the sprouts reach the surface of the soil, while green-tipped is cut above the ground and develops its colour when it comes into contact with sunlight. Before briefly steaming, boiling, griddling or roasting, trim off the woody end.

CELERY

Celery lends a crunchy texture to salads and also makes a good base for soups and stews. Green celery is available all year round, and white is available in winter. Choose stems that are very firm and rigid, but don't forget the leaves, which have a tangy flavour and can be added to stocks. Celery hearts can also be braised.

CHICORY

The long, tightly packed leaves of red or white chicory have a distinctive, bitter taste so use sparingly. Trim the root, remove the core and slice thinly. Chicory can be served raw in salads, steamed or braised.

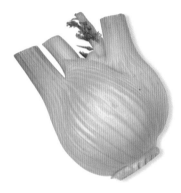

usually greyish-brown in colour, they also come in pale yellow and pink. Shiitake have a chewy texture and robust flavour, and are most commonly used in Asian dishes.

FENNEL

Fennel has a mild aniseed flavour, which is most potent when eaten raw. Roasting fennel (cut into wedges) tempers the flavour and adds a delicious sweetness. It also goes well with Mediterranean flavours such as tomatoes, olive oil, garlic and basil.

MUSHROOMS

There is a wide range of mushrooms to choose from, both fresh and dried, and even many types of wild mushroom are now cultivated. The most popular are the mild-flavoured button-capped and the field mushroom, which has a more earthy, intense flavour. Buy mushrooms that are firm and smell fresh; avoid ones that have slimy, damp patches. Dried mushrooms keep well: to reconstitute them, soak in boiling water for 20–30 minutes. Drain and rinse well to remove any dirt and grit. Use the soaking water in stocks and sauces, but sieve first.

CEPS

Ceps (or porcini) have a meaty texture and woody flavour. Dried ceps lend a rich flavour to soups, stocks and sauces.

CHANTERELLE

Golden-coloured chanterelle (or girolle) mushrooms have a delicate flavour. They should be wiped rather than washed, as they are very porous. Most types of mushroom should be prepared in this way, apart from the honeycomb-capped morel.

SHIITAKE AND OYSTER

Both shiitake and oyster mushrooms are now widely cultivated. Oyster are fluted in shape, and while they are

HOW TO PREPARE FRESH MUSHROOMS

It is best not to wash mushrooms, or you risk making them soggy and unappetizing. Instead, trim off the stalks, then wipe the caps with a piece of moistened kitchen paper to remove any soil or compost. Some mushrooms are grown in a sandy medium, which is difficult to remove by wiping. Plunge the mushrooms into a bowl of cold water and any sand will sink. Shake well before drying with kitchen paper.

ROOT VEGETABLES

The comfort foods of the vegetable world, potatoes, carrots, swede, celeriac, beetroot and parsnips, among others, have a sweet, dense flesh that provides a range of vitamins and minerals, not forgetting fibre.

POTATOES

There are hundreds of different potato varieties and many lend themselves to particular cooking methods. Waxy potatoes, like Charlotte, are best boiled, or try roasting them whole, while floury varieties, like Maris Piper, lend themselves to roasting, baking and mashing. Stored in a dark, well-ventilated place, potatoes will keep for about two weeks. Sweet potatoes have an orange or white flesh (the former is richer in beta carotene). When cooked, the white-fleshed variety has a drier texture, but both are good roasted, mashed or baked.

LETTUCES

Cos and iceberg have firm, crisp leaves, while Little Gem is a smaller, sweeter version of cos. The pretty frilly leaves of lollo rosso are green at the base and a deep red around the edge. Equally attractive is the oakleaf. Nutritionally, lettuce is best eaten raw, with the darker outer leaves containing more nutrients than the pale-coloured inner. However, it can also be braised, steamed and turned into soups.

OTHER SALAD LEAVES

Cress, mizuna, rocket and watercress have a strong, distinctive flavour and will enliven any salad. Escarole, frisée and radicchio are slightly bitter in flavour and are best used in moderation as they can easily dominate a salad.

FRUIT VEGETABLES

Tomatoes, aubergines, chillies, avocados and peppers are all vegetables, but botanically they are classified as fruit. This nutritious group adds plenty of colour and flavour to a range of dishes. Known in the Middle East as 'poor man's caviar', aubergines give substance and flavour to spicy stews and tomato-based bakes, and can be roasted, grilled or puréed into garlicky dips.

CARROTS AND BEETROOT

When buying carrots and beetroot, remember that the smaller ones are sweeter. Raw carrots and beetroot can be grated into salads or used to make relishes. Roasting them intensifies their sweetness and both work well in soups.

CELERIAC

Celeriac is a knobbly root with a flavour reminiscent of celery. Peel and grate raw into salads, steam, bake or combine with potatoes to make a delicious mash.

JERUSALEM ARTICHOKES

These small, knobbly tubers have a mild, nutty flavour and are delicious roasted or transformed into soup. Scrub rather than peel before use.

SALAD LEAVES

Salad leaves come in a huge variety of shapes, textures, colours and flavours, from the bitter-tasting endive to peppery watercress and delicate butterhead lettuce. Convenient bags of mixed salad leaves allow you to sample a wide range of different types, although they do not tend to last as long as the individually packed types.

TOMATOES

There are now so many varieties of tomato to choose, from the sweet, bite-sized cherry to the large beef. The egg-shaped plum tomato makes rich sauces, while sun-dried tomatoes add a richness to dips, sauces, soups and stews.

CHILLIES

Chillies form a crucial role in many cuisines, including Mexican, Indian and Thai. There are hundreds of different types, which range in potency from the mild and flavourful to the blisteringly hot.

PEPPERS

Red, yellow and orange peppers are an excellent source of vitamin C, the green and purple to a lesser extent. Green peppers are fully developed, but are not as ripe as their more colourful counterparts, which can make them relatively difficult to digest.

AVOCADOS

Avocados are rich in vitamins C and E and are said to improve the condition of the skin and hair. Brush with lemon or lime juice after cutting to prevent the flesh turning brown. They are usually served raw, but can also be baked.

PODS AND SEEDS

The vegetables in this category, such as peas, green beans, mangetout, sugar snap peas, broad beans and sweetcorn, all have a good nutritional value.

PEAS

Peas are one of the few vegetables that taste as good when cooked from frozen as when cooked fresh.

BROAD BEANS

Broad beans are best when very fresh and young. Tiny pods can be eaten whole, while when slightly older, you may prefer to pop the bean out of its tough shell after cooking to reveal a succulent green bean.

GREEN BEANS

When buying green beans (runner, French and dwarf), look for good colour and no sign of discolouration or wilting. Simply top and tail, then steam until just tender. They are delicious when served as a warm salad with a dressing made of ginger, garlic, sesame oil and rice wine vinegar.

SWEETCORN

These are best eaten soon after picking and after purchase, before the natural sugars have started to convert into starch and lose their sweetness and the kernels toughen. Preferably buy corn on the cob encased in its green husk, which helps to keep it fresh.

ONION FAMILY

Onions, garlic, leeks, shallots and spring onions add plenty of flavour to all manner of savoury vegetarian dishes and can also be cooked on their own. Onions and garlic should be stored in a cool, dry, airy place away from direct sunlight.

ONIONS

These provide potent antioxidants and are said to reduce health-threatening cholesterol levels in the body. Cooking tempers the pungency of the onion family, while roasting brings out their delicious sweetness. Onions offer a range of taste sensations from the sweet and mild Spanish white onion and light and fresh spring onion to the versatile and pungent yellow onion. Baby onions and shallots are the smallest.

PUMPKIN AND SQUASH

This group of vegetables comes in a wide range of colours, shapes and sizes. They are broadly divided into two types: summer, which include cucumbers, courgettes and marrows; and winter, such as the various pumpkins and squashes.

HOW TO PREPARE PUMPKIN AND SQUASH

These vegetables have thick skins, which are usually removed before cooking. Select a large, heavy knife and put a damp tea towel under the chopping board so that it doesn't slip. Cut off a slice from the bottom, to give you a flat base, and cut off the stalk end, too. Stand the vegetable on the base and cut away the tough skin with firm, vertical slices for butternut squash or following the curve for round varieties and pumpkins. Then slice in half and use a large spoon to scrape out all the seeds and fibres. Dice or slice the flesh.

SUMMER

Courgettes are at their best when small and young; the flavour diminishes the older and larger they get and the seeds toughen. Extremely versatile, courgettes can be steamed, stir-fried, puréed, griddled and roasted, as well as used in soups and casseroles. Their deep yellow flowers are perfect for stuffing. Look for firm, bright, unblemished vegetables that are heavy for their size.

WINTER

Butternut squash is one of the most readily available winter types. A large, distinctively pear-shaped vegetable with a golden skin and orange flesh, it is equally delicious mashed, baked or roasted, or used in soups and stews, and makes a good substitute for pumpkin. Small pumpkins have a sweeter, less fibrous flesh than the large ones, which are probably best kept for making lanterns at Halloween!

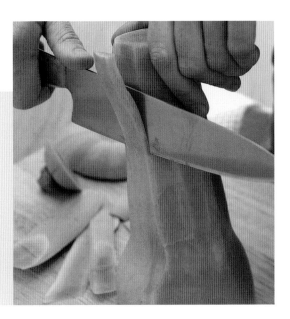

Fruit

Like vegetables, the range of fruit to choose from is incredibly diverse. It is easy to routinely buy the same types every week, but it really is worth experimenting with new varieties. The ultimate convenience food, most fruit simply needs a wash and is ready to eat. As most nutrients are found just below the skin, avoid peeling if possible and preferably eat raw rather than cooked, as the latter affects nutrient levels. Good quality and freshness is essential when buying fruit; not only will it taste better and last longer, but it will be higher in antioxidant nutrients. Buy organic whenever you can and avoid bulk-buying if the fruit is going to sit in the fruit bowl or refrigerator for days.

CITRUS FRUIT

Vibrantly coloured oranges, lemons, grapefruit, clementines and limes are packed with beneficial vitamin C and beta carotene. They make a versatile addition to the kitchen, lending themselves to both sweet and savoury dishes. Once cut or peeled, use straight away, as vitamin C levels diminish from the moment they are sliced into.

ORANGE

Popular varieties of orange include the juicy Jaffa, Valencia and navel (named after the belly button-type spot at the flower end). Thin-skinned oranges tend to be the juiciest. Marmalade is made from the sour-tasting Seville orange. Orange rind or peel adds a fragrant note to cakes, biscuits and sweet sauces, as well as savoury dishes.

LEMON

Lemons (juice and rind) are an essential ingredient in the kitchen; just a squeeze of juice will add zing to salad dressings, vegetables and marinades. The rind also enlivens both sweet and savoury dishes. Lemon juice can also prevent some fruit and vegetables, such as avocado and apples, discolouring when cut. Avoid those with green patches on the skin, as this is a sign of unripeness.

LIME

Limes have a sharper flavour than lemons and are often used in Indian, Indonesian and Thai cooking, adding a fragrant note.

HOW TO SEGMENT CITRUS FRUIT

Use a serrated knife to cut off a slice from the top and bottom of the fruit to reveal the flesh.

Remove the skin and white pith, either in a spiral, beginning at the cut top and following the curve of the fruit, or by standing the fruit on the cut base and cutting down from top to bottom around the fruit.

Hold the fruit in the palm of your hand over a bowl. Use a small fruit knife to cut in front of the membrane. Push the knife forward to remove the segment cleanly from the membrane. Cut in front of the next membrane, then again push the knife forward towards the outer edge of the fruit – the segment will drop into the bowl.

Continue to separate all the segments from the membrane, then squeeze the membrane tightly. Unless using the segments immediately, put in a small bowl, cover with clingfilm and refrigerate to prevent the air oxidizing the fruit and making it bitter.

ORCHARD FRUIT

Probably the most popular group of fruit, ranging from crisp apples to succulent peaches and juicy cherries. There are hundreds of different varieties of apple, and while we only see a mere fraction of these, many shops are now beginning to stock more unusual types. The Bramley is the most widely used cooking apple, but does require sweetening with sugar. Some eating apples are equally good stewed in a little water and no extra sugar is required.

PEACH

Gorgeous succulent peaches range in colour from gold to deep red and the flesh can be golden or white. Nectarines are similar, but without the fuzzy skin. Buy both peaches and nectarines slightly hard and then ripen them at home. They easily bruise, so care is needed.

PEAR

Like certain apples, some varieties of pear are good for cooking, while others are best eaten raw. Pears are best in the late summer and autumn with the arrival of the new season's crop. Particular favourites are the plump Comice, green-brown-skinned Conference and yellow-skinned William.

CHERRY

Glossy, sweet red cherries make a welcome appearance in stores in the summer months. There are two types: sweet and sour. The latter is best cooked.

PLUM

Plums are a popular summer fruit and vary in colour and flavour from the sweet and juicy to the slightly tart. The latter are best cooked in pies and cakes.

CURRANTS

These tiny baubles of brightly coloured fruit make a pretty addition to desserts. Blackcurrants, whitecurrants and redcurrants are usually sold in bunches on the stem. To remove the currants from the stalk, run the prongs of a fork down through the clusters, taking care not to damage the fruit. They can be on the tart side and may need a sprinkling of sugar. Currants look attractive in fruit salads, pies and summer pudding, or can be transformed into jellies and jams.

BERRIES

Usually at their best in the summer, berries are mostly available all year round.

STRAWBERRY

Strawberries, if at their peak of ripeness (avoid those with white or green tips), need little embellishment; simply a spoonful of cream or crème fraîche will suffice. Strawberries contain plenty of vitamin C, and they are a good source of B vitamins.

RASPBERRY

Raspberries are very fragile and don't have a long shelf life. Their soft, delicate texture and aromatic flavour are best suited to simple preparations.

GOOSEBERRY

Gooseberries are a popular fruit in northern Europe, but are relatively rare in other parts of the world. They range from the tart green variety with the fuzzy skin, which is best suited to pies, crumbles and jams, to the softer, sweeter, purple type. This can be mixed with cream or custard to make a fruit fool.

BLACKBERRY

Blackberries are a familiar sight in British hedgerows in early autumn, but the cultivated type have a longer season. Juicy and plump, blackberries vary in sweetness. Often used in cooking, they are delicious in summer pudding, tarts, pies, crumbles or puréed to make a sauce that goes with ice cream or nut roasts.

BLUEBERRY

Ripe blueberries are plump and slightly firm, with a natural 'bloom'. They are delicious eaten raw, but can also be made into jams and jellies and baked into pies, tarts, cakes and muffins.

GRAPES

Grapes range in colour from deep purple to pale red, and from vibrant green to almost white. Most grapes are grown for wine production; those for eating tend to be less acidic and have a thinner skin. Preferably buy organic grapes or wash well before eating. They should be plump and firm, and firmly attached to the stalk.

MELON

When buying melons, look for those that are heavy for their size, yield to gentle pressure and smell fragrant at the stem end – this is a sign of ripeness. There is a wide range to choose from, including the pinkish-red watermelon, yellow honeydew and orange-fleshed Cantaloupe. Watermelons are very low in calories due to their high water count and make a refreshing summer dessert. Avoid buying ready-cut fruit, as vitamin levels will have diminished.

TROPICAL FRUIT

This exotic collection of fruit ranges from the popular banana to the more unusual pawpaw (or papaya).

BANANA

The high starch content of bananas means that they provide plenty of energy as well as fibre, vitamins and minerals. The soft, creamy flesh can be baked whole, frozen to make a quick ice cream, blended into smoothies or mashed into cakes. Bananas with patches of green can be ripened at room temperature, but it is not advisable to buy entirely green fruit, as they rarely ripen properly.

PINEAPPLE

Pineapples have a sweet and juicy flesh. Choose fruit that are heavy for their size and are slightly tender when pressed, with fresh, green, spiky leaves. The fruit is ripe when you can successfully pull out a leaf, without tugging. Pineapples are particularly good for the digestive system.

MANGO

Mangoes have a wonderfully fragrant, juicy pulp when ripe, which can be used in a wide range of both sweet and savoury dishes, turned into smoothies, ice cream, purées and sauces, and added to salsas and salads. The skin ranges in colour from green to yellow, orange or red. A mango that is entirely green is likely to be unripe, although in Asia these are often sliced into salads.

PAWPAW

The slightly pear-shaped pawpaw (papaya) has a speckled yellow skin when ripe, a vibrant pinkish-orange pulp and an incredibly perfumed flavour. The numerous edible seeds taste peppery when dried. Pawpaw is best eaten raw, although unripe green fruit can be used in cooking.

KIWI FRUIT

Kiwi fruit or Chinese gooseberry are particularly rich in vitamin C. The puréed flesh can be used to make refreshing sorbets and ice creams. Slice in half and scoop out the green flesh and tiny black seeds with a spoon for a healthy snack or use in fruit salads.

PASSION FRUIT

Passion fruit does not look particularly inviting, with its dark, wrinkly skin, but inside is a fragrant mixture of golden pulp and edible black seeds ready to be eaten.

Grains and Cereals

When we think of grains, rice, wheat and oats immediately spring to mind, yet this group
is surprisingly wide and each type comes in various forms, from the whole grain to flour.
For most of us, grains form a major part of our diet and a nutritious one at that: high in
complex carbohydrates, grains also contain protein, fibre, vitamins and minerals, and are
low in fat. Unprocessed types, such as wholemeal bread and pasta, are richer in these
nutrients, since the refining process depletes much of their goodness. Inexpensive and
readily available, they make a versatile addition to the storecupboard.

To ensure freshness, always buy grains and their related
products from shops that have a regular turnover of stock.
Store in airtight containers in a cool, dry, dark cupboard to
prevent them becoming stale and to keep moisture out.

WHEAT
*The most widely available grain crop in the Western
world, wheat comes in various forms.*

FLOUR
Flour is ground from the wholegrain and may be wholemeal or
white, depending on the degree of processing. Strong or hard
flour is high in gluten, which makes it ideal for breadmaking,
while soft flour is lower in gluten and higher in starch, making
it better for cakes and pastries. Durum wheat flour is one of
the hardest wheat varieties and is used to make pasta.

OTHER FORMS
Other forms of wheat include wheat berries, bran, flakes,
cracked wheat, bulgar wheat, semolina, wheat grass and
couscous. The latter, which looks like a grain, is actually a form
of pasta made by steaming and drying cracked durum wheat.

RICE
*Almost every culture in the world has its own culinary
repertoire of rice dishes, ranging from Spanish paella
to Indian biryani.*

LONG-GRAIN AND BROWN RICE
Long-grain is the most widely used type of rice; brown rice
has a nutty, chewier texture than white, which contains less
fibre and fewer nutrients.

BASMATI
Basmati, available both brown and white, is a slender, long-
grain rice and is aged for a year after harvest. Widely used in
Indian dishes, its light, fluffy grain is also good for rice salads.

THAI AND JAPANESE RICE
Thai or jasmine rice has a soft, sticky texture and a mild,
perfumed flavour – which explains its other name, fragrant
rice. Japanese rice also has a soft, sticky texture and is mixed
with rice vinegar to make sushi rolls.

ARBORIO, CARNAROLI AND VALENCIA

Arborio and Carnaroli are classic risotto rices. The short, stubby grain absorbs about five times its weight in water, creating a creamy result. Valencia rice, used for paella, is also a short-grain rice, but it is not quite as starchy as risotto rice.

OTHER FORMS

Other forms to look out for are pudding rice, red rice and wild rice; the latter, with its slender black grains, is not in fact a true rice but an aquatic grass.

STORING AND REUSING COOKED RICE

Leftover cooked rice can be kept in an airtight container in the refrigerator. Make sure it is thoroughly cooled before refrigerating. If it is being used cold in salads, chill and use within a day. Reheat cooked rice thoroughly. Microwave until piping hot or tip the rice into a saucepan of boiling water and reheat it for 1 minute only, or steam it over boiling water. Cooked rice is susceptible to a bacteria, *Bacillus cereus*, which can cause stomach upsets if not used within 2 days.

OTHER GRAINS
OATS

Like rye, oats are a popular grain in Northern Europe. Flaked and rolled oats are used to make porridge and muesli. Medium and fine oatmeal is best in oatcakes and breads. Oats are believed to reduce cholesterol levels in the blood.

CORN

Also known as maize, corn comes in yellow, blue, red and even black varieties. We are most familiar with yellow corn, which is used for cornmeal or polenta, cornflour and popcorn.

RYE

Rye flour is commonly used to make a dark, dense bread, particularly in Eastern Europe, Scandinavia and Russia. The strong-tasting grain can also be used in savoury dishes.

QUINOA

This highly nutritious grain is one of the few plant foods that is a complete protein, which means it contains all eight essential amino acids. The tiny bead-type grain has a mild, slightly bitter taste and can be used to make tabbouleh, stuffings, bakes, pilafs and breakfast cereals.

MILLET

This grain is not widely used, but it is highly nutritious, containing more iron than most other grains and is a good source of zinc. The tiny bead-like grains have a mild flavour and make the perfect accompaniment to stews and curries, and can be used in pilafs, tabbouleh, milk puddings and porridge. It is also gluten-free.

BARLEY

Pearl barley is the most common form and is husked, steamed and polished to give it its characteristic ivory-coloured look. Pot barley is the whole grain and takes much longer to cook than pearl. Both types make a satisfying porridge and can be added to stews, bakes and soups.

Pulses and Beans

Lentils, beans and peas are all pulses and are an excellent source of low-fat protein as well as complex carbohydrates, vitamins, minerals and fibre. Their versatility and ability to absorb the flavours of other foods mean that they can form the base of a great number of different dishes. Although pulses can be kept for up to a year, they do tend to toughen with time. Buy from shops with a high turnover of stock and look for bright, unwrinkled pulses that are not dusty. Store pulses in an airtight container in a cool, dark place and rinse before use. Avoid adding salt to the water when cooking, as this prevents them from softening; instead, season when cooked.

LENTILS

Unlike most other pulses, lentils do not require presoaking and are relatively quick to cook. They are sold dried or canned and can be used in a variety of dishes – dahls, burgers, bakes, stews and soups.

GREEN LENTILS
Similar to the brown lentil, green lentils have a slightly milder flavour and can be cooked and blended with herbs and garlic to make a nutritious spread. The tiny, dark, grey-green Puy lentil is grown in France and is considered superior in flavour to other varieties. They take around 25–30 minutes to cook, but retain their bead-like shape. They are delicious in warm salads with a vinaigrette dressing and also make a hearty addition to stews.

DRIED PEAS
Unlike lentils, peas are soft when young and need to be dried. Available whole or split, the latter has a sweeter flavour and cooks more quickly.

YELLOW AND GREEN SPLIT PEAS
Yellow and green split peas are interchangeable with red split lentils and are perfect for dahls, soups, casseroles and purées, but they do take slightly longer to cook.

SPLIT LENTILS
Orange-coloured red lentils are the most familiar variety, and because they are 'split', they can be cooked in around 20 minutes, eventually disintegrating into a thick purée. They are ideal for thickening soups and stews, and are used to make the spicy Indian dish, dahl.

MARROW FAT PEAS
Marrow fat peas are larger in size and are used to make the British classic 'mushy' peas. They should be soaked overnight before cooking.

BROWN LENTILS
These disc-shaped lentils, sometimes called Continental lentils, have a robust texture and flavour. Available whole, they take longer to cook than red lentils – around 45 minutes – and add substance to stews, stuffings and soups.

BEANS

With the exception of the ubiquitous baked bean, beans are often ignored, yet they are all so versatile, lending themselves to pies, bakes, stews, soups, pâtés, dips, burgers, salads and more. What often puts people off is the long soaking time – usually overnight – but canned beans are just as good and incredibly convenient. Just drain and rinse before use.

CHICKPEAS

Chickpeas resemble shelled hazelnuts and have a nutty flavour and a creamy texture. They are widely used in Indian and Middle Eastern cuisines. In India, they are ground to make the yellow-coloured gram flour, which is used for making fritters and flatbreads.

FLAGEOLET AND BORLOTTI

The pretty, pale green flageolet bean has a fresh, delicate taste and soft texture, while the hearty borlotti bean is pinkish-brown in colour with a sweetish flavour and tender texture, often used to make Italian bean and pasta soups.

CANNELLINI

Cannellini beans are white, kidney-shaped beans, which have a soft, creamy texture when cooked. They are equally delicious served warm in salads or puréed to make a tasty, nutritious alternative to mash.

RED KIDNEY

Red kidney beans have a soft, 'mealy' texture and retain their colour and shape when cooked. They are used to make Mexican refried beans and are essential to a successful chilli.

HARICOT

Haricot beans (navy or Boston beans) are most commonly used for canned baked beans, but the ivory-coloured bean is also good in stews and soups.

BUTTER AND LIMA

Butter and lima beans are similar in flavour and appearance. These cream-coloured, kidney-shaped beans have a soft, floury texture.

SOYA BEANS

This versatile bean has all the nutritional properties of animal products, but none of the disadvantages. They range in colour from creamy yellow through to brown-black and make a healthy addition to soups, casseroles and bakes. The dried beans are very dense and need to be soaked for 12 hours before cooking.

Soya beans are also used to make tofu, tempeh, meat-replacement mince and chunks, flour, soya milk, soy sauce and miso, as well as a range of sauces, including black bean sauce, yellow bean sauce and hoisin sauce.

COOKING BEANS

Once soaked, beans should be drained and rinsed in clean water. Any pulses that have floated to the surface during soaking should be discarded. You need to allow plenty of water for cooking: 1.2 litres/2 pints fresh cold water per 450 g/1 lb beans. Bring to the boil over a high heat and boil for 10 minutes, then reduce the heat and simmer until the beans are soft but not mushy, which can take anything from 30 minutes to 2 hours, depending on the type and age of the bean. The beans must always be submerged: top up with boiling water to keep them covered by about 1 cm/½ inch as necessary. The cooking water can be used as a vegetable stock. If you are cooking more than one variety of bean, they need to be soaked and cooked separately, as they will cook at different rates. Remember to add salt only towards the end of cooking.

Dairy Products

Dairy produce provides vegetarians with valuable protein as well as calcium and vitamins D and B, including B12. Many dairy products are high in fat and therefore should be eaten sparingly, or alternatively, you can opt for reduced-fat alternatives. For those who do not eat dairy products, there are an increasing number of substitutes to choose from, which have similar culinary properties.

MILK, CREAM AND YOGURT

YOGURT
The fat content of yogurt ranges from 0.5 g per 100 g through to 10 g per 100 g for thick Greek-style yogurt. Although the latter is higher in fat than most types of yogurt, it is lower in fat than cream and makes a useful replacement in cooking, as it does not curdle, unlike low-fat varieties. Live or bio yogurts have been fermented with beneficial bacteria that can aid digestion and have a mild, creamy flavour.

MILK
Cow's milk is one of our most widely used ingredients, but skimmed and semi-skimmed versions now outsell their full-fat counterpart, yet they are not nutritionally inferior. Organic milk is now widely available, and comes from cows that have been fed a pesticide-free diet and are not routinely treated with hormones. For those who are intolerant of cow's milk, there is goat's and sheep's milk, which are nutritionally similar, but easier to digest.

CREAM
The fat content of cream varies enormously, ranging from about 12 per cent for half-fat through to a decadent 55 per cent for clotted cream. Crème fraîche is a rich, cultured cream with a fat content of around 35 per cent, yet now comes in half-fat versions (around 10 per cent). A spoonful adds a delicious creaminess to sauces or dolloped onto fresh fruit, especially strawberries. Soured cream is treated with lactic acid, which gives it its characteristic tang. It contains 20 per cent fat, although it is possible to buy reduced-fat versions. If using in cooking, take care that it does not curdle.

NON-DAIRY ALTERNATIVES
It is important for vegans in particular to ensure their diet includes the protein, minerals and vitamins found in dairy products. The best source is the soya bean. Tofu, or soya cheese, made from cooked soya beans, is an excellent non-meat protein that is cholesterol-free. As well as being a useful source of calcium, tofu also contains vitamin E, manganese, phosphorus and iron. Milk, cream, and yogurt products are also made from dried soya beans.

Other products that are nutritionally similar to cow's milk are milk and cheese substitutes made from oats, rice and nuts. Pure vegetable margarines and spreads are also available.

FRESH UNRIPENED CHEESES

Young, immature cheeses are unlikely to contain rennet and have a light, mild flavour.

COTTAGE CHEESE

Cottage cheese is a soft, fresh-curd variety of cheese and is available in large- and small-curd varieties. Cottage cheese is one of the most popular and is lower in fat – 2–5 per cent – than most other cheeses.

FROMAGE FRAIS

Fromage frais is a smooth, fresh cheese with the same consistency as thick yogurt, but is less acidic. The fat content varies from almost nothing to about 8 per cent. It can be used in much the same way as yogurt.

ITALIAN RICOTTA

The Italian ricotta can be made from sheep's or cow's milk and has a slightly granular texture. Its mild, clean flavour means that it can be used in both savoury and sweet dishes.

CREAM CHEESE AND QUARK

Cream cheese has a rich, velvety consistency, while Quark is a low-fat curd cheese. Both are perfect for making cheesecakes, dips and spreads.

FRESH RIPENED CHEESES

BRIE AND CAMEMBERT

These fresh, soft, cow's milk cheeses predominantly come from France. When fully ripe, they have an invitingly buttery texture that 'oozes' inside. Camembert tends to have a stronger flavour than Brie, which is enhanced when served at room temperature.

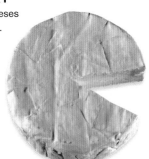

OTHER SOFT AND HARD CHEESES

The following gives just a taster of other soft and hard cheeses that are all readily available in vegetarian rennet versions.

MOZZARELLA

Mozzarella has a delicate, silky texture, as well as excellent melting properties, hence its use on pizzas and bakes. It is usually made from cow's milk, but the traditional cheese is made from buffalo's milk and is called mozzarella di bufala.

HALLOUMI

Halloumi has been called the vegetarian alternative to bacon. It has a firm, rubbery texture and salty flavour; cut it into slices and grill or griddle.

FETA

Feta can be soaked in water for 10 minutes to remove its saltiness. It has a firm, crumbly texture and is used in the classic Greek salad. It was once made with goat's or sheep's milk, but is now more often made with cow's milk.

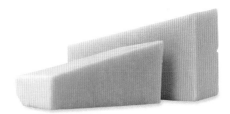

CHEDDAR

Cheddar is a national favourite, but it varies tremendously in quality. Look for mature or vintage traditional farmhouse Cheddar, which is aged between nine and 24 months and has a rich, almost nutty flavour.

Nuts and Seeds

Nuts and seeds are more than just a convenient snack, making a useful and healthy addition to both sweet and savoury vegetarian dishes. Best bought in small quantities from shops with a high turnover of goods, nuts and seeds can become rancid – especially shelled ones. Stored in an airtight container in a cool, dark place, nuts and seeds should last about three months.

NUTS

Nuts are the fruits of trees, with the exception of peanuts, which grow underground. Although fairly high in fat, it is the beneficial omega-6 type, and they also provide a range of other nutrients, including protein, B vitamins, iron, selenium, vitamin E and zinc. Nuts are available whole, with or without shells, blanched, flaked, chopped, ground or toasted.

BRAZIL NUTS
Brazil nuts have a sweet, milky taste and are particularly rich in omega-6 essential fatty acids. They are often used in muesli-type breakfast cereals or in desserts.

MACADAMIA NUTS
Macadamia nuts have a creamy, rich, buttery flavour and a surprisingly high fat content. The round nut is usually sold shelled, as the outer casing is extremely hard to crack.

ALMONDS
Almonds come in two types: bitter and sweet. The former is not recommended raw, but is transformed into a fragrant oil and essence. Sweet almonds are best bought shelled in their skins. You can blanch them yourself in boiling water for a few minutes to remove the skin. However, you can also buy them ready-blanched as well as flaked, toasted and ground, all of which add a richness and pronounced flavour to cakes, desserts and some savoury dishes.

CASHEW NUTS
Cashew nuts are always sold without their tough outer shell and are lower in fat than most other nuts. Their creamy flavour lends itself to roasts, bakes and nut butters, or they add a pleasant crunch when in noodle dishes and salads.

HAZELNUTS
The versatile hazelnut is sold whole, shelled, chopped and ground, and is especially good roasted. Use in both savoury and sweet dishes.

CHESTNUTS
Cooked or roasted chestnuts have a delicious sweet taste and floury texture. They add substance to stuffings, roasts, bakes and pies. Sweetened chestnut purée is used in desserts.

PINE KERNELS
The pine kernel is one of the key ingredients in pesto and the tiny, cream-coloured nut has a rich, creamy flavour, which is enhanced by toasting. Buy in small quantities as their high fat content means that they readily become rancid.

WALNUTS

When picked young, walnuts are referred to as 'wet' and have a fresh, milky kernel. However, they are usually bought dried – shelled, chopped or ground – when the nut adopts a slightly bitter flavour.

COCONUT

Coconut is high in saturated fat, so is best eaten in moderation. Coconut milk and cream add a rich creaminess to sauces, curries, smoothies, desserts and soups. The dense white 'meat' is also made into desiccated or flaked coconut.

SEEDS

Albeit tiny, seeds pack a powerful punch when it comes to their nutritional status. They are a good source of the antioxidant vitamin E and iron, as well as the essential fatty acid omega-6, which may help in reducing harmful cholesterol levels – and all that from a small and unassuming seed!

SESAME SEEDS

Tiny sesame seeds come in black or white and are used to make a surprising range of products. Ground into a thick paste, they make tahini; the base of hummus; the sweet confection halva; or are turned into a rich, toasted oil. Their flavour is improved by toasting in a dry frying pan until golden. Sprinkle over salads, noodles, bakes, cakes and breads.

SUNFLOWER SEEDS

Toasting also improves the flavour of sunflower seeds, but take care not to burn them, as their nutritional content will be affected. The tear-shaped seeds have similar uses to sesame seeds and make a healthy addition to salads, breakfast cereals and flapjacks.

PUMPKIN SEEDS

Pumpkin seeds are one of the few plant foods to contain both omega-3 and omega-6 essential fatty acids and are richer in iron than other seeds. They make a nutritious snack or can be used in much the same way as other seeds.

POPPY SEEDS

The small, black poppy seed adds an attractive decorative look as well as crunch to breads and cakes. They are used in German and Eastern European pastries, strudels and tarts.

LINSEEDS

Long known for its oil, used to polish wood, these small, golden seeds are also known as flaxseed. Linseeds are one of the few vegetarian sources of omega-3 essential fatty acids and can be sprinkled over breakfast cereals and salads or mixed into breads and pastries.

HOW TO TOAST NUTS AND SEEDS

To remove the papery husk from hazelnuts or almonds, simply put the nuts on a baking tray and heat in a preheated oven at 180°C/350°F/Gas Mark 4 for 5–10 minutes to loosen the skins. Remove, and when the nuts are cool enough to handle, rub off the skins in a clean tea towel.

Seeds and nuts, such as whole or flaked almonds, are also toasted to enhance their flavour. Smaller quantities of seeds can be toasted in a dry frying pan until they change colour, but for larger amounts, spread the seeds or nuts in a single layer on a baking tray and roast in a preheated oven at 180°C/350°F/Gas Mark 4 for 5–7 minutes.

Herbs and Spices

Highly revered for thousands of years, herbs and spices can enliven even the simplest of dishes. Invaluable ingredients in the vegetarian kitchen, they enhance the aroma and flavour of both savoury and sweet dishes. Both also have a positive effect on the digestive system. Although the following concentrates on fresh herbs, dried can make a useful alternative, especially during the winter months when some fresh herbs are not available.

HERBS

Fresh herbs are now sold loose, in pots or packets. It is possible to enhance the shelf life of the latter by removing the herbs from the packet and immersing the stems in a jar of water. Cover with a polythene bag, then seal with an elastic band; the herbs should keep for up to a week.

BASIL

Basil is a popular fresh herb and is commonly used in Italian dishes, especially pesto. The purple variety is widely used in Thai cooking. The fragile leaves are best torn rather than cut with a knife to prevent them bruising. Drying basil impairs its taste and so is not recommended.

CORIANDER

Another favourite in Thai cooking, the warm and spicy flavour of coriander also enlivens Indian dishes. The root is edible and can be ground into Indian and Thai curry pastes.

MINT

There are numerous varieties of mint, peppermint and spearmint being the most readily available. Mint can be mixed with natural yogurt to make raita, a calming accompaniment to hot curries; immersed in hot water to make a refreshing mint tea; or used in the fragrant salad, tabbouleh.

DILL

Dill is a scented herb. The feather-like leaves of the plant are used as a herb, while the seeds come from the flower heads after they have matured.

TARRAGON

Tarragon is popular in French cooking and has an affinity with egg and cheese dishes.

CHIVES

Chives are a part of the onion family, but have a milder flavour that works best when sprinkled over salads, eggs and tomato-based dishes as a garnish.

BAY

The attractive, glossy green leaves of the bay tree add a robust, spicy flavour to stocks and stews, and are used to make bouquet garni.

OREGANO

Oregano is one of the few fresh herbs that dries well. Closely related to marjoram, but with a more robust flavour, oregano especially complements tomato-based dishes. Both oregano and thyme work well in marinades and are largely interchangeable in their uses.

PARSLEY

Both flat-leaf and curly-leaf parsley are commonly available in shops. Flat-leaf looks similar to coriander and is preferable in cooking to the curly type.

SAGE, ROSEMARY AND THYME

Sage is pungent in flavour, but can work well with nut roasts, bakes and stews. Rosemary has a strong and aromatic flavour and works best in hearty soups and stews. Thyme has a strong piquant or lemony flavour.

SPICES

Spices – the seeds, fruit, pods, bark and buds of plants – should be bought in small quantities from a shop with a regular turnover of stock. Aroma is the best indication of freshness, as this diminishes when a spice is stale. Store spices in airtight jars away from direct sunlight.

GINGER

Ginger has a warming, slightly peppery flavour that is quite different to the fresh root. It is used to flavour cakes, breads and biscuits, but is also added to curries, stews and soups.

CARDAMOM

Pungent, warm and aromatic, the spice known as cardamom is derived from several plants. It is sold as a seed pod or ground as a spice.

CUMIN AND CORIANDER

A key component in Middle Eastern, North African and Indian cooking, cumin comes both ground and in whole seed form. Black seeds, also known as nigella, have a sweeter and milder flavour than the brown seeds. Ground coriander is used in much the same way as cumin, while the ivory-coloured whole seeds are often used as a pickling spice as well as ground in curries and tagines.

CINNAMON, NUTMEG AND CLOVES

These have a wonderfully warming flavour and are often used together in cakes, puddings and biscuits. Whole cinnamon sticks (quills) flavour curries, pilafs and fruit compotes.

SAFFRON

Saffron is the world's most expensive spice. Made from the dried stigmas of *Crocus sativus*, only a tiny amount is required to add a distinctive flavour and a golden colour to paella, stews and milky puddings.

PEPPER

Pepper is undoubtedly the most widely used spice and comes in a multitude of colours – black, white, pink and green. The spice not only adds its own flavour to dishes, but brings out the flavour of other ingredients.

CAYENNE AND PAPRIKA

Cayenne is a fiery spice that adds colour and flavour to curries, soups and stews. Paprika is milder and can be used more liberally. Both are said to be good for the circulation.

VANILLA

Vanilla pods provide a fragrant, mellow, sweet taste, with a rich, perfumed aroma. They are often used in sweet dishes.

HOW TO FREEZE HERBS

Herbs must be in perfect condition before they are frozen: anything stale, bruised or contaminated will not be improved by freezing.

Wash the herbs carefully and shake dry. Lay out on kitchen paper to dry completely, then transfer to a tray and open freeze in a single layer. Once frozen, pack into small bags or boxes and use as required.

Alternatively, chop the washed and dried herbs (they will bruise and blacken if they are not dry) and pack into ice-cube trays to half fill. Top up with water and freeze. Drop the herb ice cubes into stews, soups and casseroles for an instant herb seasoning.

Get Cooking

While most vegetables can be eaten raw, there are numerous cooking techniques to add interest and variety to vegetarian meals. You want to maximize flavour, colour and texture, while preserving as much of the essential vitamins and nutrients as possible. Since vegetables are so central to your diet, it pays to consider how best to cook them.

FRESHLY PREPARED...

The fresher the ingredients, the higher their nutrient content. Avoid old, tired, wilted vegetables and do not store anything for long at home. It is far better to buy fresh and loose when you need them, and to select organic if you can, in preference to ready-prepared packs, which will have lost some of their vitamins as well as their flavour. If possible, avoid peeling vegetables, because many nutrients are stored close to or in the skin (or put the peelings into a pot to make stock). Wash or scrub everything, but don't leave vegetables soaking in water or their soluble nutrients will leach out. Similarly, do not cut or prepare vegetables too far in advance, as some vitamins, such as vitamin C, diminish once the cut surface is exposed to the air.

BOILING

The traditional way to cook vegetables is to use plenty of salted water and a large, uncovered saucepan. This method is most suitable for sweetcorn, potatoes and other root vegetables. Although steaming is preferable when cooking green vegetables because they retain more nutrients, if you choose to boil them leave them uncovered; put the lid on and they lose their attractive bright green colour. Choose an appropriate-sized saucepan for the amount of vegetables so that the water can circulate, but use the minimum amount of water, cook for the briefest period and drain the vegetables immediately, because boiling destroys water-soluble vitamins, such as B and C. Other soluble nutrients leach into the cooking water, so get into the habit of keeping the cooking water and use it as a base for soup or sauces.

right *When boiling broccoli keep the lid off the saucepan to preserve the colour.*

POACHING

A less vigorous way to cook more delicate vegetables is to put them in boiling liquid (water, stock, wine or milk), then to simmer them gently over a low heat to retain their flavour, texture and shape.

FRYING

Deep-frying is less popular these days, with concerns over the amount of fat in our diet. In fact, if the cooking temperature is correct, deep-fried foods are quickly sealed and absorb less oil than when they are shallow-fried. Coating vegetables in batter or in egg and breadcrumbs forms a crispy seal, which also reduces oil absorption. Deep-frying is a long-established cooking method for potatoes (chips) and also works well for aubergines and courgettes. Dry-frying in a frying pan or in a ridged griddle pan or on a flat griddle plate is a healthier option that can be used for some vegetables as well as halloumi cheese.

STEAMING

Unlike boiling, less water comes into contact with steamed vegetables, so they are crisper and retain more essential nutrients. Also, some vegetables – mangetout, leeks and courgettes – become limp and unappetizing if boiled. Steamed new potatoes are particularly delicious; try putting some fresh mint leaves under the potatoes to flavour them while they are steaming.

COOKING TIMES

For maximum nutritional benefit, it makes sense to cook your vegetables for the least time possible. Cut them the same size so that they look attractive and cook evenly. While potatoes have to be cooked right through, other root vegetables, such as carrots, are best served with a little 'bite' to them. Boil for less time or steam your vegetables and enjoy the extra crunch. Some vegetables – those with a high water content such as spinach, celery or beansprouts – need only be blanched in boiling water for 30 seconds.

For frying or stir-frying, ensure that the oil is properly hot before adding the vegetables. When time is short, try microwaving your vegetables. This method requires less liquid or fat as well as shorter cooking times than conventional cooking.

below *When braising, brown the vegetables before adding only a little water and cook slowly.*

BRAISING

This cooking method requires only a very little water, and the saucepan is covered. The heat is much reduced and the cooking time greatly increased. You can start by browning the ingredients in a little oil or butter, then add water or other liquid before covering the saucepan. The small amount of liquid that remains at the end of cooking will be sweet and flavoured – serve the vegetables with this juice and you gain all the nutrients. Onions, white turnips, leeks, chicory, celery and fennel lend themselves to braising. Red cabbage is one of the brassicas that positively benefits from this long, slow treatment.

left *Roast vegetables in a roasting tin with olive oil and herbs to add extra flavour.*

below *Sautée vegetables slowly in a frying pan without a lid, using only a little olive oil.*

STIR-FRYING

This method of frying in a little oil over a very high heat has become widely popular. Stir-fried vegetables retain far more of their nutritional value, flavour, texture and colour. Typically, vegetables are very thinly sliced and rapidly moved around in a hot wok to aid fast and even cooking. Most of us are familiar with stir-fried baby sweetcorn, mangetout, peppers, beansprouts and bamboo shoots, but the method is an equally good way to cook thinly sliced cauliflower, Brussels sprouts, cabbage and carrots.

ROASTING

Traditionally, roasting vegetables meant cooking them in the fat dripping from a joint of meat. A far healthier vegetarian option is to roast vegetables lightly drizzled with olive oil in a roasting tin, to which you can add garlic and herbs for additional flavour. Roast squash, parsnips, onions, tomatoes, asparagus and even beetroot are all delicious; the flavour is concentrated and the natural sweetness accentuated.

SAUTÉEING AND SWEATING

These methods use less oil than traditional shallow-frying and are longer, slower processes than stir-frying. Sautéeing is done in an uncovered frying pan; sweating in either a heavy-based casserole or frying pan, covered, so that water from the ingredients is trapped and falls back into the pan. Onions are often sweated to soften but not colour.

BAKING

Potatoes, onions and garlic can be baked 'dry' in their skins, while softer vegetables (peppers and tomatoes) can be stuffed with rice and other fillings or foil-wrapped.

GRILLING AND BARBECUING

The intense heat from a grill or charcoal is unsuitable for either delicate or dense vegetables, which only become charred not cooked, but excellent for softer ones, such as onions, sweetcorn, aubergines and tomatoes. All vegetables need to be brushed with oil before being placed on the grill.

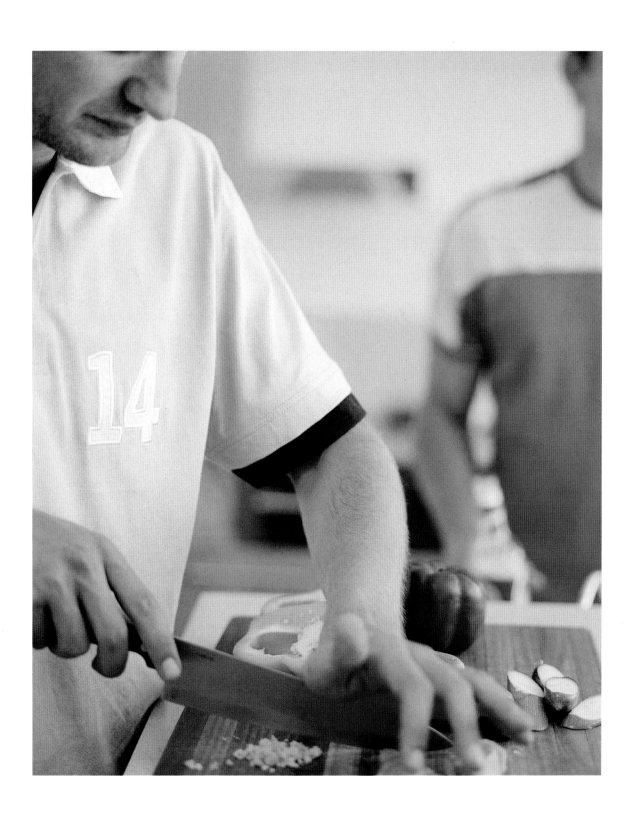

Basic Recipes

The recipes in this book provide a wide variety of delicious vegetarian meals. Some of them incorporate a common basic recipe, to which you can refer on these pages, or you can use these basic recipes as an addition to a dish of your choice.

CHEESE SAUCE
Makes: 600 ml/1 pint

VEGETABLE STOCK
Makes: 2 litres/3½ pints

2 tbsp sunflower or corn oil
115 g/4 oz onions, finely chopped
115 g/4 oz leeks, finely chopped
115 g/4 oz carrots, finely chopped
4 celery sticks, finely chopped
85 g/3 oz fennel, finely chopped
85 g/3 oz tomatoes, finely chopped
2.25 litres/4 pints water
1 bouquet garni

Heat the oil in a large saucepan over a low heat. Add the onions and leeks and cook, stirring frequently, for 5 minutes, or until softened.

Add the remaining vegetables, cover and cook over a very low heat, stirring occasionally, for 10 minutes. Add the water and bouquet garni and bring to the boil, then reduce the heat and simmer for 20 minutes.

Sieve, leave to cool, then cover and store in the refrigerator. Use within 3 days or freeze in portions for up to 3 months.

40 g/1½ oz butter
5 tbsp plain flour
600 ml/1 pint milk
140 g/5 oz grated Cheddar cheese
salt and pepper

Melt the butter in a saucepan over a medium heat. Stir in the flour and cook, stirring constantly, for 1–2 minutes.

Remove from the heat and gradually whisk in the milk. Return to the heat and bring to the boil, whisking constantly. Simmer for 2 minutes, or until the sauce is thick and glossy. Remove from the heat, add the cheese and stir until melted. Season to taste with salt and pepper.

TOMATO SAUCE
Makes: 150 ml/5 fl oz

1 tbsp olive oil
1 small onion, chopped
1 garlic clove, chopped
400 g/14 oz canned chopped
  tomatoes
2 tbsp chopped fresh parsley
1 tsp dried oregano
2 bay leaves
2 tbsp tomato purée
1 tsp sugar
salt and pepper

Heat the oil in a saucepan over a medium heat. Add the onion and cook, stirring, for 2–3 minutes until beginning to soften.

Add the garlic and cook, stirring, for 1 minute. Stir in the tomatoes, parsley, oregano, bay leaves, tomato purée and sugar and season to taste with salt and pepper.

Bring the sauce to the boil, then reduce the heat and simmer, uncovered, for 15–20 minutes until the sauce has reduced by half. Remove and discard the bay leaves just before serving.

PESTO SAUCE
Makes: 75 ml/2½ fl oz

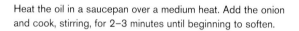

55 g/2 oz fresh basil
  leaves
15 g/½ oz pine kernels
1 garlic clove
pinch of salt
25 g/1 oz freshly grated Parmesan cheese
3 tbsp extra virgin olive oil

Put the basil leaves, pine kernels, garlic and salt in a mortar and pound to a paste with a pestle.

Transfer to a bowl and, with a wooden spoon, gradually work in the Parmesan cheese, followed by the oil, to make a thick, creamy sauce.

Cover with clingfilm and refrigerate until required.

MAYONNAISE
Makes: 300 ml/10 fl oz

2 egg yolks
pinch of salt, plus extra for seasoning
150 ml/5 fl oz sunflower oil
150 ml/5 fl oz olive oil
1 tbsp white wine vinegar
2 tsp Dijon mustard
pepper

Beat the egg yolks with the pinch of salt in a bowl.

Whisk the oils together in a jug. Gradually add one quarter of the oil mixture to the egg yolks, a drop at a time, beating constantly with a whisk or electric mixer.

Beat in the vinegar, then continue adding the oils in a steady stream, beating constantly.

Once all the oil has been incorporated, stir in the mustard and season to taste with salt and pepper.

TZATZIKI
Makes: 500 ml/18 fl oz

500 ml/18 fl oz natural Greek-style yogurt or other
  thick natural yogurt
4 garlic cloves, very finely chopped
2 cucumbers, peeled, deseeded and very finely diced
1 tbsp lemon-flavoured or extra virgin olive oil
3 tbsp lemon juice
1 tbsp chopped fresh mint leaves
salt and pepper
paprika, to garnish

TO SERVE
celery batons
carrot batons
pitta bread triangles

Put the yogurt, garlic, cucumber, oil, lemon juice and mint in a serving bowl and stir together until well combined. Season to taste with salt and pepper, cover with clingfilm and chill in the refrigerator for at least 2 hours, or until required.

When ready to use, garnish with a little paprika. Serve with celery and carrot batons and pitta bread triangles for dipping.

RICH SHORTCRUST PASTRY DOUGH
Makes: 1 x 23-cm/9-inch flan

175 g/6 oz plain flour
pinch of salt
85 g/3 oz butter, diced, plus extra for greasing
1 egg yolk
3 tbsp ice-cold water

Sift the flour with the salt into a bowl. Add the butter and rub into the flour with your fingertips until the mixture resembles fine breadcrumbs.

Beat the egg yolk with the water in a small bowl. Sprinkle the liquid over the flour mixture and combine with a round-bladed knife or your fingertips to form a dough. Shape the dough into a ball, wrap in foil and chill in the refrigerator for 30 minutes.

PIZZA DOUGH BASES

Makes: 2 x 25-cm/10-inch pizzas

225 g/8 oz plain flour, plus extra for dusting
1 tsp salt
6 tbsp lukewarm water
2 tbsp olive oil, plus extra for oiling
1 tsp easy-blend dried yeast

Sift the flour with the salt into a large, warmed bowl and make a well in the centre. Add the water, oil and yeast to the well. Using a wooden spoon or your hands, gradually mix in, drawing the flour from the side, to form a dough.

Turn out onto a lightly floured work surface and knead for 5 minutes, or until smooth and elastic. Form the dough into a ball, put in a clean, lightly oiled bowl and cover with oiled clingfilm. Leave in a warm place to rise for 1 hour, or until doubled in size.

Turn out the dough onto a lightly floured work surface and knock back. Knead briefly before shaping into 2 pizza bases.

PUFF PASTRY

Makes: 1 x 25-cm/10-inch flan or pie

175 g/6 oz plain flour, plus extra for dusting
pinch of salt
175 g/6 oz unsalted butter
about 150 ml/5 fl oz ice-cold water

Sift the flour with the salt into a large bowl. Dice 25 g/ 1 oz of the butter and rub into the flour with your fingertips. Gradually add the water, just enough to bring the dough together, and knead briefly to form a smooth dough. Wrap the dough in foil and chill in the refrigerator for 30 minutes.

Keep the remaining butter out of the refrigerator, wrap in foil and shape into a 3-cm/1¼-inch thick rectangle. Roll out the dough on a lightly floured work surface to a rectangle 3 times longer and 3 cm/1¼ inches wider than the butter, unwrap the butter and put in the centre of the dough, long-side towards you. Fold over the 2 'wings' of pastry to enclose the butter, press down the edges with the rolling pin to seal and then turn the pastry so that the short side faces you. Roll out the pastry to its original length, fold into 3, turn and roll again to its original length.

Repeat this once more, then rewrap the pastry and chill again for 30 minutes. Repeat the rolling and turning twice more. Chill again for 30 minutes. At this point you can freeze the pastry until you need it.

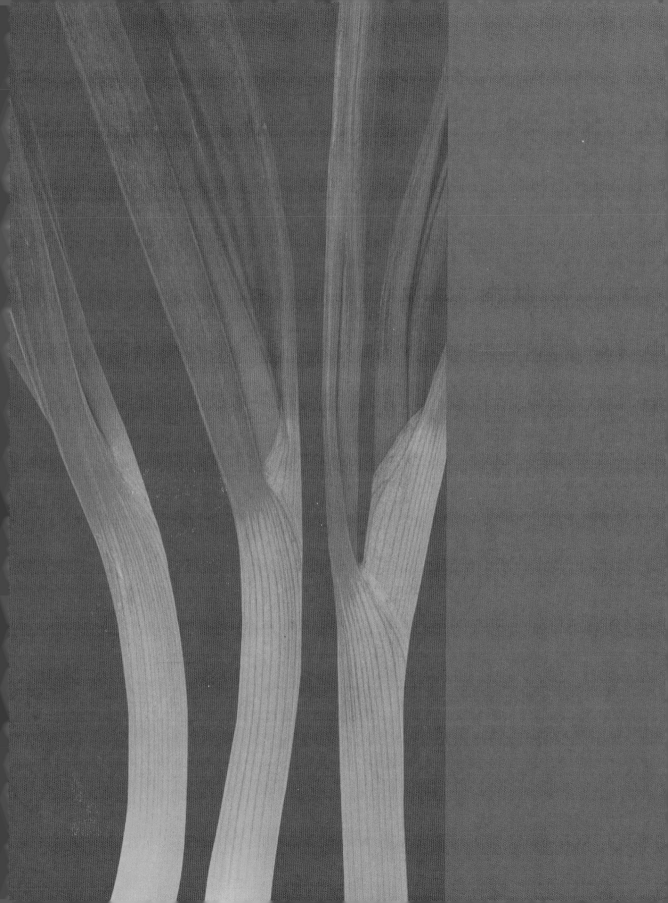

2

Home-made soups provide a powerhouse of nutrients as well as a wealth of flavours, and you can be sure that they aren't overloaded with salt, unlike so many of even the better quality commercially produced varieties. What's more, they are surprisingly quick and easy to make.

SOUPS

Whether you want a soup that's hearty and chunky or something more luxurious and smooth – perhaps a light, fragrant broth as a prelude to an Asian-style meal or even a chilled soup you are sure to find a recipe to fit the bill. The collection includes such great vegetarian classics as Vichyssoise, Gazpacho, French Onion Soup and Borscht.

serves 6 | prep 40 mins, plus 4–8 hrs' chilling | cook 35 mins

vichyssoise

INGREDIENTS
450 g/1 lb leeks, white parts only
450 g/1 lb potatoes
55 g/2 oz butter
1.2 litres/2 pints water
600 ml/1 pint milk
300 ml/10 fl oz soured cream, plus extra
** to garnish**
salt and pepper
2 tbsp snipped fresh chives, to garnish

Thinly slice the leeks. Peel and dice the potatoes. Melt the butter in a large, heavy-based saucepan over a very low heat. Add the leeks, cover and cook, stirring occasionally, for 10 minutes.

Stir in the potatoes and cook over a medium heat, stirring frequently, for 2 minutes. Pour in the water and add a pinch of salt. Bring to the boil, then reduce the heat and simmer for 15–20 minutes until the potatoes are tender. Remove from the heat and leave to cool slightly. Transfer to a blender or food processor and process into a purée. Push the mixture through a sieve into a clean saucepan with a wooden spoon, then stir in the milk. Season to taste with salt and pepper and stir in half the soured cream.

Reheat the soup, then push through a sieve into a bowl. Stir in the remaining cream, cover with clingfilm and leave to cool. Chill in the refrigerator for 4–8 hours. Serve in chilled bowls, with swirls of soured cream and chives to garnish.

COOK'S TIP
For a more intense flavour, you can use a vegetable bouillon powder or stock cube mixed with the water.

serves 4–6 | prep 20 mins, plus 4 hrs' chilling | no cooking required

gazpacho

INGREDIENTS

**500 g/1 lb 2 oz large, juicy tomatoes, peeled,
  deseeded and chopped**
**3 large, ripe red peppers, cored, deseeded
  and chopped**
2 tbsp sherry vinegar, or to taste
4 tbsp olive oil
pinch of sugar
salt and pepper

TO SERVE

ice cubes
finely diced red pepper
finely diced green pepper
finely diced yellow pepper
finely diced deseeded cucumber
finely chopped hard-boiled eggs
croûtons fried in garlic-flavoured olive oil

Put the tomatoes, chopped red peppers, vinegar, oil and sugar in a blender or food processor and process until blended and as smooth or chunky as you like. Transfer to a bowl, cover and chill for at least 4 hours before serving. Taste and adjust the seasoning, adding extra vinegar, if necessary.

To serve, ladle the soup into bowls and add 1–2 ice cubes to each. Put the other accompaniments in bowls and let everyone add their own.

> **COOK'S TIP**
> *Cold dulls flavours, so more
> seasoning will be needed
> than for a soup served
> warm. For this reason, taste
> and adjust the seasoning
> after chilling the soup.*

serves 3–4 | prep 5 mins, plus 4 hrs' chilling | cook 5 mins

chilled pea soup

INGREDIENTS
425 ml/15 fl oz vegetable stock or water
450 g/1 lb frozen peas
55 g/2 oz spring onions, chopped, plus extra
** to garnish**
300 ml/10 fl oz natural yogurt or single cream
salt and pepper

TO GARNISH
2 tbsp chopped fresh mint or snipped fresh chives
grated lemon rind

Bring the stock to the boil in a large saucepan over a medium heat. Reduce the heat, add the peas and spring onions and simmer for 5 minutes.

Leave to cool slightly, then sieve twice, making sure that you remove and discard any pieces of skin. Pour into a large bowl, season to taste with salt and pepper and stir in the yogurt. Cover the bowl with clingfilm and chill in the refrigerator for several hours.

To serve, mix the soup well and ladle into a large tureen or individual soup bowls or mugs. Garnish with chopped mint or snipped chives, spring onions and grated lemon rind.

serves 6 | prep 30 mins | cook 1½ hrs

french onion soup

INGREDIENTS

675 g/1 lb 8 oz onions
3 tbsp olive oil
4 garlic cloves, 3 chopped and
  1 peeled but kept whole
1 tsp sugar
2 tsp chopped fresh thyme, plus extra sprigs
  to garnish
2 tbsp plain flour
125 ml/4 fl oz dry white wine
2 litres/3½ pints vegetable stock
6 slices French bread
300 g/10½ oz Gruyère cheese, grated

VARIATION

*If desired, you can stir
2 tablespoons brandy into
the soup just before
ladling it into the bowls.*

COOK'S TIP

*Make sure that you allow
yourself plenty of time to
make the vegetable stock
in advance of making the
soup. If the stock is left to
stand, the flavours will
have time to develop.*

Thinly slice the onions. Heat the oil in a large,
heavy-based saucepan over a medium–low heat,
add the onions and cook, stirring occasionally,
for 10 minutes, or until they are just beginning
to brown. Stir in the chopped garlic, sugar and
chopped thyme, then reduce the heat and cook,
stirring occasionally, for 30 minutes, or until the
onions are golden brown.

Sprinkle in the flour and cook, stirring constantly,
for 1–2 minutes. Stir in the wine. Gradually stir in
the stock and bring to the boil, skimming off any
scum that rises to the surface, then reduce the
heat and simmer for 45 minutes. Meanwhile,
preheat the grill to medium–hot. Toast the bread
on both sides under the grill, then rub the toast
with the whole garlic clove.

Ladle the soup into 6 flameproof bowls set on a
baking tray. Float a piece of toast in each bowl
and divide the grated cheese between them.
Place under the grill for 2–3 minutes, or until the
cheese has just melted. Garnish with thyme sprigs
and serve at once.

serves 8 | prep 30 mins, plus 4 mins' standing | cook 1 hr 40 mins

genoese vegetable soup

INGREDIENTS

2 onions, sliced

2 carrots, diced

2 celery sticks, sliced

2 potatoes, peeled and diced

115 g/4 oz French beans, cut into
 2.5-cm/1-inch lengths

115 g/4 oz peas, thawed if frozen

200 g/7 oz fresh spinach leaves, coarse stems
 removed, shredded

2 courgettes, diced

225 g/8 oz Italian plum tomatoes, peeled,
 deseeded and diced

3 garlic cloves, thinly sliced

4 tbsp extra virgin olive oil

2 litres/3½ pints vegetable stock

1 quantity pesto sauce

140 g/5 oz dried stellete or other soup pasta

salt and pepper

freshly grated Parmesan cheese, to serve

COOK'S TIP

*To peel tomatoes, cut a
cross in the base of each
and put in a heatproof bowl.
Cover with boiling water and
leave for 30–45 seconds.
Drain and plunge into cold
water, then the skins will
slide off easily.*

Put the onions, carrots, celery, potatoes, beans, peas, spinach, courgettes, tomatoes and garlic in a large, heavy-based saucepan over a medium–low heat, pour in the extra virgin olive oil and stock and bring to the boil. Reduce the heat and simmer gently, stirring occasionally, for 1½ hours.

Meanwhile, make the pesto sauce. Cover with clingfilm and refrigerate until required.

Season the soup to taste with salt and pepper and add the pasta. Cook for a further 8–10 minutes until the pasta is tender but still firm to the bite. The soup should be very thick.

Stir in half the pesto sauce, remove from the heat and leave to stand for 4 minutes. Taste and adjust the seasoning, adding more salt, pepper and pesto sauce, if necessary. (Any leftover pesto sauce may be stored in a screw-top jar in the refrigerator for up to 2 weeks.)

Ladle into warmed bowls and serve at once. Hand round the extra Parmesan cheese separately.

serves 4 | prep 20 mins | cook 10 mins

chinese vegetable soup

INGREDIENTS

115 g/4 oz Chinese leaves
2 tbsp groundnut oil
225 g/8 oz marinated tofu, cut into
  1-cm/½-inch cubes
2 garlic cloves, thinly sliced
4 spring onions, thinly sliced diagonally
1 carrot, thinly sliced
1 litre/1¾ pints vegetable stock
1 tbsp Chinese rice wine
2 tbsp light soy sauce
1 tsp sugar
salt and pepper

Shred the Chinese leaves and reserve. Heat the oil in a large preheated wok or frying pan over a high heat. Add the tofu cubes and stir-fry for 4–5 minutes until browned. Remove from the wok with a slotted spoon and drain on kitchen paper.

Add the garlic, spring onions and carrot to the wok and stir-fry for 2 minutes. Pour in the stock, rice wine and soy sauce, then add the sugar and shredded Chinese leaves. Cook over a medium heat, stirring, for a further 1–2 minutes until heated through.

Season to taste with salt and pepper and return the tofu to the wok. Ladle the soup into warmed bowls and serve.

VARIATION

If you are unable to find Chinese rice wine, substitute dry sherry. You can also use firm lettuce leaves, such as Little Gem or cos, instead of Chinese leaves.

serves 4 | prep 10 mins, plus 1 hr soaking | cook 5 mins

hot-&-sour soup

INGREDIENTS

6 dried shiitake mushrooms

115 g/4 oz dried rice vermicelli noodles

**4 small fresh green chillies, deseeded
   and chopped**

6 tbsp rice wine vinegar

850 ml/1½ pints vegetable stock

2 lemon grass stalks, snapped in half

**115 g/4 oz canned water chestnuts, drained,
   rinsed and halved**

6 tbsp Thai soy sauce

juice of 1 lime

1 tbsp palm sugar or soft light brown sugar

3 spring onions, chopped, to garnish

Put the dried mushrooms in a heatproof bowl and pour in enough boiling water to cover. Set aside to soak for 1 hour. Meanwhile, put the noodles in a separate heatproof bowl and pour in enough boiling water to cover. Set aside to soak for 10 minutes. Combine the chillies and vinegar in a third bowl and set aside.

Drain the mushrooms and noodles. Bring the stock to the boil in a large saucepan over a high heat. Add the mushrooms, noodles, lemon grass, water chestnuts, soy sauce, lime juice and sugar and return to the boil.

Stir in the chilli and vinegar mixture and cook for 1–2 minutes. Remove and discard the lemon grass. Ladle the soup into warmed bowls and serve hot, garnished with spring onions.

serves 4–6 | prep 10 mins | cook 40 mins

tomato soup

INGREDIENTS
900 g/2 lb large, juicy tomatoes, halved
2 tbsp butter
1 tbsp olive oil
1 large onion, sliced
**2–3 tbsp tomato purée, depending on the
  flavour of the tomatoes**
850 ml/1½ pints vegetable stock
2 tbsp amontillado sherry
½ tsp sugar
salt and pepper
crusty bread, to serve

TO GARNISH
parsley, chopped
150 ml/5 fl oz single cream (optional)

COOK'S TIP
*If you don't possess a mouli,
purée the soup in a blender
or food processor, then work
through a fine sieve to
achieve the smooth texture.*

Preheat the grill to high. Put the tomatoes,
cut-sides up, on a baking tray and grill about
10 cm/4 inches from the heat for 5 minutes, or
until just starting to char on the edges.

Meanwhile, melt the butter with the oil in a large
saucepan or flameproof casserole over a medium
heat. Add the onion and cook, stirring frequently,
for 5 minutes. Stir in the tomato purée and cook
for a further 2 minutes.

Add the tomatoes, stock, sherry, sugar and salt
and pepper to taste to the saucepan and stir.
Bring to the boil, then reduce the heat to low
and simmer, covered, for 20 minutes, or until the
tomatoes are reduced to a pulp.

Process the soup through a mouli into a large
bowl. Return to the rinsed-out saucepan and
simmer, uncovered, for 10 minutes, or until the
desired consistency is achieved. Ladle into
individual bowls. Cool and serve chilled, if desired,
decorating with swirls of cream and garnishing
with parsley. Serve with plenty of bread.

serves 4–6 | prep 10 mins | cook 25 mins

leek & potato soup

INGREDIENTS
55 g/2 oz butter
1 onion, chopped
3 leeks, sliced
225 g/8 oz potatoes, peeled and cut into
 2-cm/¾-inch cubes
850 ml/1½ pints vegetable stock
salt and pepper

TO GARNISH
150 ml/5 fl oz single cream (optional)
2 tbsp snipped fresh chives

Melt the butter in a large saucepan over a
medium heat, add the vegetables and cook,
stirring frequently, for 2–3 minutes until slightly
softened. Pour in the stock and bring to the
boil, then reduce the heat, cover and simmer,
stirring occasionally, for 15 minutes.

Remove from the heat and leave to cool
slightly. Using a hand-held stick blender, blend
the soup until smooth, or transfer to a blender
or food processor and process until smooth.
Return to the rinsed-out saucepan.

Reheat the soup, season to taste with salt and
pepper and serve in warmed bowls, garnished
with swirls of cream, if desired, and chives.

herbed potato
& cheddar soup

INGREDIENTS

1½ tbsp vegetable oil
1 garlic clove, chopped
1 large onion, chopped
2 potatoes, peeled and chopped
1 large carrot, chopped
1 bay leaf
600 ml/1 pint vegetable stock
25 g/1 oz butter, softened
2 tbsp chopped fresh parsley
2 tbsp snipped fresh chives
100–115 g/3½–4 oz fresh crusty bread,
   lightly toasted
90 g/3¼ oz Cheddar cheese, coarsely grated
salt and pepper

Heat the oil in a large saucepan over a medium–low heat. Add the garlic and onion and cook, stirring frequently, for 4 minutes until slightly softened. Add the potatoes and carrot and cook, stirring frequently, for a further 5 minutes. Add the bay leaf and stock and season to taste with salt and pepper. Bring to the boil, then reduce the heat, cover and simmer, stirring occasionally, for 25 minutes, or until the vegetables are tender.

Meanwhile, put the butter in a small bowl and beat in half the parsley and half the chives. Spread onto the toasted bread and top with the cheese.

Cut into small chunks about 2.5-cm/1-inch square and set aside. Remove and discard the bay leaf from the soup.

Leave the soup to cool slightly, then transfer to a blender or food processor and process for 1 minute, or until smooth. Return to the rinsed-out saucepan, stir in the remaining herbs and reheat gently. Ladle into bowls, divide the chunks of bread between the bowls and serve.

serves 4 | prep 20 mins | cook 15 mins

sweetcorn, potato & cheese soup

INGREDIENTS
25 g/1 oz butter
2 shallots, finely chopped
225 g/8 oz potatoes, peeled and diced
4 tbsp plain flour
2 tbsp dry white wine
300 ml/10 fl oz milk
325 g/11½ oz canned sweetcorn kernels, drained
85 g/3 oz Gruyère, Emmenthal or
  Cheddar cheese, grated
8–10 fresh sage leaves, chopped, plus extra
  sprigs to garnish
425 ml/15 fl oz double cream

CROUTONS
2–3 slices day-old white bread
2 tbsp olive oil

To make the croûtons, cut the crusts off the bread slices, then cut the bread into 5-mm/ ¼-inch squares. Heat the oil in a heavy-based frying pan over a high heat, add the bread cubes and cook, tossing and stirring constantly, until evenly coloured. Remove with a slotted spoon, drain thoroughly on kitchen paper and set aside.

Melt the butter in a large, heavy-based saucepan over a low heat. Add the shallots and cook, stirring frequently, for 5 minutes, or until softened. Add the potatoes and cook, stirring, for 2 minutes.

Sprinkle in the flour and cook, stirring constantly, for 1 minute. Remove from the heat and stir in the wine. Return to the heat and gradually stir in the milk. Bring to the boil, stirring constantly, then reduce the heat to a simmer.

Stir in the sweetcorn, cheese, chopped sage and cream and heat through gently until the cheese has just melted. Ladle the soup into warmed bowls and scatter over the croûtons. Garnish with sage sprigs and serve at once.

COOK'S TIP
When you are cooking croûtons, make sure that the oil is very hot before adding the bread cubes, otherwise the cubes may turn out soggy rather than crisp.

serves 4 | prep 15 mins | cook 40 mins

hearty lentil & vegetable soup

INGREDIENTS

2 tbsp vegetable oil

3 leeks, green parts included, finely sliced

3 carrots, diced

2 celery sticks, quartered lengthways and diced

115 g/4 oz brown or green lentils

75 g/2¾ oz long-grain rice

1 litre/1¾ pints vegetable stock

8 corn on the cob quarters

salt and pepper

TO GARNISH

4 tbsp snipped fresh chives

150 ml/5 fl oz soured cream

Heat the oil in a large saucepan over a medium heat. Add the leeks, carrots and celery, cover and cook, stirring occasionally, for 5–7 minutes until just tender. Stir in the lentils and rice.

Stir in the stock. Bring to the boil, then reduce the heat, cover and simmer over a medium–low heat for 20 minutes. Add the corn on the cob and simmer, covered, for a further 10 minutes, or until the lentils and rice are tender.

Season the soup to taste with salt and pepper. Ladle into individual warmed bowls, sprinkle with chives and top with a spoonful of soured cream. Serve at once.

serves 6 | prep 30 mins | cook 1¼ hrs

borscht

INGREDIENTS

1 onion
55 g/2 oz butter
350 g/12 oz raw beetroot, cut into thin batons,
  and 1 raw beetroot, grated
1 carrot, cut into thin batons
3 celery sticks, thinly sliced
2 tomatoes, peeled, deseeded and chopped
1.4 litres/2½ pints vegetable stock
1 tbsp white wine vinegar
1 tbsp sugar
2 large fresh dill sprigs, including to garnish
115 g/4 oz white cabbage, shredded
salt and pepper
150 ml/5 fl oz soured cream, to garnish
rye bread, to serve (optional)

Slice the onion into rings. Melt the butter in a large, heavy-based saucepan over a low heat. Add the onion and cook, stirring frequently, for 5 minutes until softened. Add the beetroot batons, carrot, celery and tomatoes and cook, stirring frequently, for 4–5 minutes.

Snip the dill sprigs. Add the stock, vinegar, sugar and a tablespoon of dill into the saucepan. Season to taste with salt and pepper. Bring to the boil, then reduce the heat and simmer for 35–40 minutes until the vegetables are tender.

Stir in the cabbage, cover and simmer for a further 10 minutes. Stir in the grated beetroot, with any juices, and cook for a further 10 minutes. Ladle into warmed bowls. Garnish with a spoonful of soured cream and another tablespoon of snipped dill and serve with rye bread, if desired.

COOK'S TIP

It is not essential to add extra beetroot towards the end of cooking, but this helps to provide the spectacular purple colour of the soup and also freshens the flavour.

VARIATION

For a more substantial soup, add 2 diced potatoes with the cabbage to the saucepan. Cook for a further 10 minutes before adding the grated beetroot.

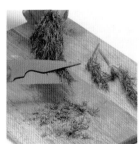

serves 4 | prep 15 mins | cook 25–30 mins

watercress soup

INGREDIENTS
**2 bunches of watercress, about 200 g/7 oz,
  thoroughly washed**
40 g/1½ oz butter
2 onions, chopped
225 g/8 oz potatoes, peeled and roughly chopped
1.2 litres/2½ pints vegetable stock or water
whole nutmeg, for grating (optional)
125 ml/4 fl oz crème fraîche, to garnish
salt and pepper

Remove the leaves from the stalks of the watercress and set side. Roughly chop the stalks.

Melt the butter in a large saucepan over a medium heat, add the onion and cook, stirring frequently, for 4–5 minutes until softened but not browned.

Add the potatoes and mix well with the onion. Stir in the watercress stalks and stock.

Bring to the boil, then reduce the heat, cover and simmer for 15–20 minutes until the potato is tender.

Stir in the watercress leaves and heat through. Remove from the heat and leave to cool slightly. Using a hand-held stick blender, blend the soup until smooth, or transfer to a blender or food processor and process until smooth. Return to the rinsed-out saucepan.

Reheat the soup, season to taste with salt and pepper and add a good grating of nutmeg, if desired. Serve in warmed bowls with the crème fraîche spooned on top.

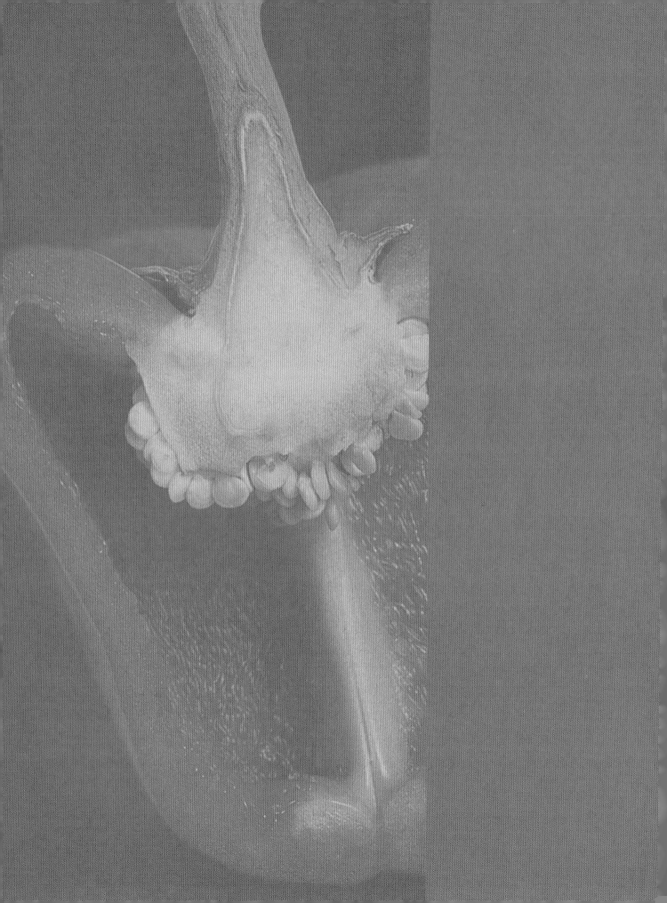

3

Colour and texture abound in this enticing range of recipes, which exploit to the full those characteristic virtues of what we still consider as essentially Mediterranean vegetables, such as aubergines, courgettes, peppers and sun-dried tomatoes, flavoured with garlic, basil and oregano.

STARTERS
& LIGHT MEALS

There are other culinary influences to sample and savour, however, from fiery Mexican Vegetable Fajitas to Chinese-style Sweet & Sour Vegetables with Cashew Nuts. You can also indulge in some comfort-food favourites, including creamy Cauliflower Cheese, Indian-spiced Bean Burgers and crisp-baked Potato Skins with Tomato & Sweetcorn Salsa.

serves 4 | prep 20 mins, plus 9½ hrs' marinating | cook 15 mins

antipasti

INGREDIENTS
450 g/1 lb large mushrooms
5 garlic cloves
about 400 ml/14 fl oz extra virgin olive oil
1 tbsp finely chopped fresh rosemary
225 ml/8 fl oz dry white wine
3 red peppers
3 orange peppers
4 tbsp fresh basil leaves
pinch of chilli powder
grated rind of 1 lemon
225 g/8 oz black olives
2 tbsp chopped fresh parsley
salt and pepper

Slice the mushrooms and put in a large serving dish. Chop 1 garlic clove. Heat 4 tablespoons of the oil in a small saucepan over a medium heat. Add the chopped garlic, rosemary and wine and bring to the boil. Reduce the heat and simmer for 3 minutes. Season to taste with salt and pepper. Pour the wine mixture over the mushrooms. Leave to cool, stirring occasionally. Cover with clingfilm and leave to marinate in the refrigerator for 8 hours.

Meanwhile, preheat the grill to medium–high. Cook the peppers under the grill, turning frequently, until the skins are blackened. Transfer to a bowl, cover and leave to cool, then peel, halve and deseed. Cut the flesh into strips. Put in a clean serving dish. Slice the remaining garlic and add to the dish with the basil. Season to taste with salt, add enough of the remaining oil to cover and toss lightly. Cover with clingfilm and leave to marinate in the refrigerator for 8 hours.

Meanwhile, heat the remaining oil, or about 125 ml/4 fl oz, in a saucepan over a low heat. Add the chilli powder and lemon rind and cook, stirring, for 2 minutes. Add the olives and cook, stirring, for 1 minute. Transfer to a clean serving dish, sprinkle with the parsley and leave to cool. Cover and leave to marinate in the refrigerator for 8 hours. Remove the antipasti from the refrigerator 1 hour before serving.

COOK'S TIP
Plan to make these antipasti
a day before you will need
them. This way, you can
leave the dishes to marinate
in the refrigerator overnight.

serves 4 | prep 15 mins | cook 10 mins

felafel with tahini sauce

INGREDIENTS
450 g/1 lb canned haricot beans, drained
350 g/12 oz canned chickpeas, drained
1 onion, finely chopped
2 garlic cloves, chopped
1 small fresh red chilli, deseeded and chopped
1 tsp baking powder
25 g/1 oz fresh parsley, chopped, plus extra
  sprigs to garnish
pinch of cayenne
2 tbsp water
vegetable oil, for deep-frying
salt and pepper

TAHINI SAUCE
200 ml/7 fl oz tahini
1 garlic clove, chopped
1–2 tbsp water
2–3 tsp lemon juice

TO SERVE
pitta bread
thick natural yogurt or tzatziki
lemon wedges

To make the tahini sauce, put the tahini and garlic in a bowl. Gradually stir in the water until a fairly smooth consistency is reached, then stir in lemon juice to taste. Add more water or lemon juice, if necessary. Cover with clingfilm and chill in the refrigerator until required.

To make the felafel, rinse and drain the beans and chickpeas. Put them in a food processor with the onion, garlic, chilli, baking powder, chopped parsley and cayenne pepper. Process to a rough paste, then add the water and season with plenty of salt and pepper. Process again briefly.

Heat about 6 cm/2½ inches of oil in a deep-fat fryer, large, heavy-based saucepan or wok over a high heat. Fry rounded tablespoonfuls of the mixture in batches for 2–2½ minutes until golden and crispy on the outside. Remove with a slotted spoon and drain well on kitchen paper. Serve hot or cold, garnished with parsley sprigs and accompanied by the tahini sauce, pitta bread, yogurt or tzatziki and lemon wedges.

serves 4 | prep 10 mins | cook 10 mins

cheese & sun-dried tomato toasts

INGREDIENTS
2 sfilatini loaves
175 ml/6 fl oz sun-dried tomato paste
300 g/10½ oz mozzarella di bufala, drained
  and diced
1½ tsp dried oregano
2–3 tbsp olive oil
pepper

Preheat the grill to high and preheat the oven
to 220°C/425°F/Gas Mark 7. Slice the loaves
diagonally and discard the end pieces. Toast the
slices on both sides under the grill until golden.

Spread one side of each toast with the sun-dried
tomato paste and top with mozzarella. Sprinkle
with oregano and season to taste with pepper.

Put the toasts on a large baking sheet and
drizzle with oil. Bake in the preheated oven for
5 minutes, or until the cheese is melted and
bubbling. Remove the toasts from the oven
and leave to stand for 5 minutes before serving.

COOK'S TIP
*If you are unable to find
sfilatini, use a large ciabatta
loaf instead and cut the
slices in half.*

serves 4 | prep 15 mins | cook 20–30 mins

stuffed aubergines

INGREDIENTS
8 small aubergines
2 tbsp vegetable or groundnut oil
4 shallots, finely chopped
2 garlic cloves, crushed
2 fresh red chillies, deseeded and chopped
1 courgette, roughly chopped
115 g/4 oz creamed coconut, chopped
few fresh Thai basil leaves, chopped
small handful of fresh coriander, chopped
4 tbsp Thai soy sauce

TO SERVE
rice with chopped spring onions
sweet chilli sauce

Preheat the oven to 200°C/400°F/Gas Mark 6. Put the aubergines on a roasting tin and cook in the preheated oven for 8–10 minutes until just softened. Cut in half and scoop out the flesh, reserving the shells.

Heat the oil in a preheated wok or large frying pan, add the shallots, garlic and chillies and stir-fry for 2–3 minutes. Add the courgettes, aubergine flesh, coconut, herbs and soy sauce and simmer, stirring frequently, for 3–4 minutes.

Divide the mixture between the aubergine shells. Return to the oven for 5–10 minutes until heated through and serve at once, accompanied by rice with spring onions and sweet chilli sauce.

COOK'S TIP
If you can only find large aubergines, one half per person would probably be enough.

serves 4 | prep 15 mins | cook 1¼ – 2¼ hrs

middle eastern baked aubergines

INGREDIENTS
300 ml/10 fl oz olive oil
450 g/1 lb onions, thinly sliced
6 garlic cloves, thinly sliced
400 g/14 oz canned chopped tomatoes
pinch of sugar
1 tsp salt
2 tbsp chopped fresh parsley
2 tbsp chopped fresh basil
2 aubergines
juice of 1 lemon
lemon wedges, to garnish

Preheat the oven to 160°C/325°F/Gas Mark 3. Heat 4 tablespoons of the oil in a large frying pan over a high heat. Add the onions and garlic, then reduce the heat to medium–low and cook, stirring frequently, until softened but not browned. Add the tomatoes and bring to the boil, then reduce the heat and simmer for 5 minutes. Add the sugar, salt and herbs.

Cut the aubergines in half lengthways. Put in a large ovenproof dish, cut-side up. Spoon the onion and tomato mixture over the top. Sprinkle with lemon juice and pour over the remaining oil. Add enough water just to cover the topping, then cover the dish and bake in the preheated oven for 1–2 hours until soft. Check frequently during the cooking time, pressing down or adding more water, if necessary.

Remove from the oven, but leave in the dish to cool. To serve, transfer to a serving dish and serve warm or at room temperature, garnished with lemon wedges.

serves 4 | prep 5 mins | cook 1 hr 5 mins

greek beans

INGREDIENTS
400 g/14 oz canned haricot
beans, drained and rinsed
1 tbsp olive oil
3 garlic cloves, crushed
425 ml/15 fl oz vegetable stock
1 bay leaf
2 fresh oregano sprigs
1 tbsp tomato purée
juice of 1 lemon
1 small red onion, chopped
25 g/1 oz stoned black olives, halved
salt and pepper

Put the beans in a flameproof casserole over a low heat, add the oil and garlic and cook, stirring frequently, for 4–5 minutes.

Add the stock, bay leaf, oregano, tomato purée, lemon juice and onion and stir well to mix. Cover and simmer for 1 hour, or until the sauce has thickened.

Stir in the olives, then season to taste with salt and pepper. The dish is delicious served either warm or cold.

COOK'S TIP
You can substitute other canned beans for the haricot beans – try cannellini or black-eyed beans, or chickpeas. Drain and rinse them before use, because canned beans often have sugar or salt added.

serves 6 | prep 15 mins | cook 1 hr 50 mins

frijoles

INGREDIENTS

2 fresh green chillies

**350 g/12 oz dried red kidney beans, soaked in
cold water for 3 hours**

2 onions, chopped

2 garlic cloves, chopped

1 bay leaf

2 tbsp sunflower or corn oil

2 tomatoes, peeled, deseeded and chopped

salt

Chop the chillies. Drain the beans and put in a
saucepan. Add enough water to cover by 2.5 cm/
1 inch, half the onion, half the garlic, the chillies
and bay leaf. Bring to the boil and boil vigorously
for 15 minutes, then reduce the heat and simmer
for 30 minutes, adding more boiling water if the
mixture begins to dry out.

Add half the oil and simmer for a further
30 minutes, adding more boiling water, if
necessary. Season to taste with salt and simmer
for a further 30 minutes, but do not add any
more water.

Meanwhile, heat the remaining oil in a frying pan.
Add the remaining onion and garlic and cook,
stirring frequently, for 5 minutes, or until softened.
Stir in the tomatoes and cook for a further
5 minutes. Add 3 tablespoons of the cooked
beans to the tomato mixture, mash thoroughly
into a paste, then stir the paste into the remaining
beans. Heat through gently, then serve.

COOK'S TIP

*Some dried pulses,
including red kidney beans,
contain a toxin that is
destroyed only by rapid
cooking. It is essential to
boil the beans vigorously
for 15 minutes, before
simmering to finish cooking.*

vegetable fajitas

INGREDIENTS

2 tbsp corn oil
2 onions, thinly sliced
2 garlic cloves, finely chopped
2 green peppers, deseeded and sliced
2 red peppers, deseeded and sliced
4 fresh green chillies, deseeded and sliced
2 tsp chopped fresh coriander
12 wheat tortillas
225 g/8 oz mushrooms, sliced
salt and pepper

Heat the oil in a heavy-based frying pan over a low heat. Add the onions and garlic and cook, stirring occasionally, for 5 minutes, or until softened. Stir in the peppers, chillies and coriander and cook, stirring occasionally, for 10 minutes.

Meanwhile, heat a separate, dry frying pan over a medium–high heat, add a tortilla and heat for 30 seconds on each side. Remove from the pan and keep warm in a low oven while you heat the remaining tortillas. Alternatively, put the tortillas in a stack and heat in a microwave oven according to the packet instructions.

Add the mushrooms to the vegetable mixture and cook, stirring constantly, for 1 minute. Season to taste with salt and pepper. Divide the vegetables between the tortillas, roll up and serve at once.

VARIATION

If you don't like dishes too spicy, use 2 fresh chillies instead of 4, or omit them altogether. The fajitas are good served with natural yogurt or soured cream.

COOK'S TIP

Always wash your hands thoroughly after handling chillies and avoid touching your lips or eyes. If you have sensitive skin, wear rubber gloves.

serves 2–3 | prep 15 mins | cook 1 hr

stuffed peppers

INGREDIENTS

6 tbsp olive oil, plus a little extra for rubbing
2 onions, finely chopped
2 garlic cloves, crushed
140 g/5 oz Spanish short-grain rice
55 g/2 oz raisins
55 g/2 oz pine kernels
40 g/1½ oz fresh parsley, finely chopped
**1 tbsp tomato purée dissolved in 700 ml/1¼ pints
  hot water**
**4–6 red, green or yellow peppers, or a mix of
  colours, or 6 of the long, Mediterranean variety**
salt and pepper

Heat the oil in a shallow, heavy-based, flameproof casserole over a medium heat. Add the onions and cook, stirring frequently, for 3 minutes. Add the garlic and cook, stirring, for a further 2 minutes, or until the onion is softened but not browned.

Add the rice, raisins and pine kernels and stir until well coated in the oil. Add half the parsley and salt and pepper to taste, then stir in the dissolved tomato purée and bring to the boil. Reduce the heat and leave to simmer, uncovered, shaking the casserole frequently, for 20 minutes, or until the rice is tender, the liquid is absorbed and small holes appear on the surface – watch carefully because the raisins can catch and burn easily. Stir in the remaining parsley, then set aside and leave to cool slightly.

Meanwhile, preheat the oven to 200°C/400°F/ Gas Mark 6. Cut the top off each pepper and reserve. Remove and discard the core and seeds from each pepper.

Divide the stuffing equally between the peppers. Use wooden cocktail sticks to secure the tops back in place. Lightly rub each pepper with oil and arrange in a single layer in a baking dish. Bake in the preheated oven for 30 minutes, or until the peppers are tender. Serve hot or leave to cool to room temperature.

COOK'S TIP

If you are using the pointed, Mediterranean variety of pepper, a melon baller, teaspoon or small paring knife makes it easier to remove all the seeds.

serves 4 | prep 20 mins | cook 35–40 mins

stuffed mushrooms

INGREDIENTS

12 large mushrooms

3 tbsp dry white wine

3 tbsp water

1 shallot, chopped

1 fresh thyme sprig, finely chopped

2 tsp lemon juice

15 g/½ oz butter

2 tsp olive oil

1 garlic clove, finely chopped

**175 g/6 oz fresh spinach leaves, tough stalks
  removed, chopped**

55 g/2 oz feta cheese, crumbled

salt and pepper

Preheat the oven to 180°C/350°F/Gas Mark 4.
Remove and finely chop the mushroom stalks.

Pour the wine and water into a wide saucepan
and add half the shallot and the thyme. Bring to
the boil over a medium heat, then reduce the heat
and simmer for 2 minutes. Add the mushroom
caps, smooth-side down, and sprinkle over the
lemon juice. Cover and simmer for 6 minutes, then
remove the mushrooms and place on a plate to
drain. Return the liquid to the boil, add the
mushroom stalks and butter and season to taste
with salt. Cook for 6 minutes, or until the liquid
has been absorbed. Transfer the stalks to a bowl.

Heat the oil in a clean saucepan over a medium
heat. Add the remaining shallot, garlic and spinach
and sprinkle with a little salt. Cook, stirring, for
3 minutes, or until all the liquid has evaporated.
Stir the spinach mixture into the mushroom stalks,

season to taste with pepper, then gently stir in the
feta cheese.

Divide the spinach mixture evenly between the
mushroom caps. Put in a single layer in an
ovenproof dish and bake in the preheated oven for
15–20 minutes until golden. Serve warm.

serves 4 | prep 10 mins | cook 1 hr 10 mins

stuffed baked potatoes

INGREDIENTS

900 g/2 lb baking potatoes, scrubbed
2 tbsp vegetable oil
1 tsp coarse sea salt
115 g/4 oz butter
1 small onion, chopped
115 g/4 oz grated Cheddar cheese or crumbled
  blue cheese
salt and pepper

OPTIONAL

4 tbsp canned, drained sweetcorn kernels
4 tbsp cooked mushrooms, courgettes or peppers

snipped fresh chives, to garnish

Preheat the oven to 190°C/375°F/Gas Mark 5. Prick the potatoes in several places with a fork and put on a baking tray. Brush with the oil and sprinkle with the salt. Bake in the preheated oven for 1 hour, or until the skins are crispy and the insides are soft when pierced with a fork.

Meanwhile, melt 1 tablespoon of the butter in a small frying pan over a medium–low heat. Add the onion and cook, stirring occasionally, for 8–10 minutes until soft and golden. Set aside.

Cut the potatoes in half lengthways. Scoop the flesh into a large bowl, leaving the skins intact. Reserve the skins. Increase the oven temperature to 200°C/400°F/Gas Mark 6.

Roughly mash the potato flesh and mix in the onion and remaining butter. Add salt and pepper to taste and stir in any of the optional ingredients, if using. Spoon the mixture back into the reserved potato skins. Top with the cheese.

Cook the filled potato skins in the oven for 10 minutes, or until the cheese has melted and is beginning to brown. Garnish with chives and serve at once.

serves 4 | prep 20 mins | cook 1 hr 10 mins

potato skins
with tomato & sweetcorn salsa

INGREDIENTS
2 large baking potatoes
85 g/3 oz canned sweetcorn kernels
55 g/2 oz canned kidney beans
2 tbsp olive oil, plus extra for brushing
115 g/4 oz tomatoes, deseeded and diced
2 shallots, finely sliced
¼ red pepper, finely diced
1 fresh red chilli, deseeded and finely chopped
1 tbsp chopped fresh coriander leaves
1 tbsp lime juice
55 g/2 oz Cheddar cheese, grated
salt and pepper
lime wedges, to garnish

Preheat the oven to 200°C/400°F/Gas Mark 6.
Prick the potatoes in several places with a fork
and brush with oil. Cook directly on the oven shelf
for 1 hour, or until the skins are crispy and the
insides are soft when pierced with a fork.

Meanwhile, make the salsa. Drain the sweetcorn
and beans, rinse well, then drain again. Put in a
bowl with the oil, tomatoes, shallots, red pepper,
chilli, coriander, lime juice and salt and pepper to
taste and mix well together.

Preheat the grill to medium. Cut the potatoes in
half lengthways. Scoop out the flesh (reserve for
use in another recipe), leaving the skins intact.
Brush the insides with oil, then put on a baking
tray, cut-sides up. Cook under the grill for
5 minutes, or until crisp.

Spoon the salsa into the potato skins and sprinkle
the cheese over the top. Return the filled potato
skins to the grill and cook gently until the cheese
has melted. Serve at once, garnished with
lime wedges.

bean burgers

INGREDIENTS
1 tbsp sunflower oil, plus extra for brushing
1 onion, finely chopped
1 garlic clove, finely chopped
1 tsp ground coriander
1 tsp ground cumin
115 g/4 oz button mushrooms, finely chopped
425 g/15 oz canned pinto or red kidney beans,
  drained and rinsed
2 tbsp chopped fresh flat-leaf parsley
plain flour, for dusting
salt and pepper

TO SERVE
burger buns
salad

Heat the oil in a heavy-based frying pan over a medium heat. Add the onion and cook, stirring frequently, for 5 minutes, or until softened. Add the garlic, coriander and cumin and cook, stirring, for a further minute. Add the mushrooms and cook, stirring frequently, for 4–5 minutes until all the liquid has evaporated. Transfer to a bowl.

Put the beans in a small bowl and mash with a potato masher. Stir into the mushroom mixture with the parsley and season to taste with salt and pepper.

Preheat the grill to medium–high. Divide the mixture equally into 4 portions, dust lightly with flour and shape into flat, round patties. Brush with oil and cook under the grill for 4–5 minutes on each side. Serve in burger buns with salad.

COOK'S TIP
If the burgers do not hold together when you try to shape them, add just a little more oil to the mixture to make them easier to handle.

serves 4 | prep 15 mins | cook 15 mins

cauliflower cheese

INGREDIENTS

1 cauliflower, cut into florets, about
  675 g/1 lb 8 oz prepared weight
40 g/1½ oz butter
40 g/1½ oz plain flour
450 ml/16 fl oz milk
115 g/4 oz Cheddar cheese, finely grated
whole nutmeg, for grating
1 tbsp freshly grated Parmesan cheese
salt and pepper

TO SERVE (OPTIONAL)
sliced tomatoes
green salad
crusty bread

Bring a large saucepan of salted water to the boil, add the cauliflower and cook for 4–5 minutes – it should still be firm. Drain, place in a hot 1.4-litre/ 2½-pint gratin dish and keep warm.

Melt the butter in the rinsed-out saucepan over a medium heat and stir in the flour. Cook for 1 minute, stirring constantly.

Remove from the heat and gradually stir in the milk until smooth.

Return to a medium heat and cook, stirring constantly, until the sauce comes to the boil and thickens. Reduce the heat to low and simmer gently, stirring constantly, for 3 minutes, or until the sauce is creamy and smooth.

Remove from the heat and stir in the Cheddar cheese and a good grating of the nutmeg. Taste and season well with salt and pepper.

Preheat the grill to high. Pour the hot sauce over the cauliflower, top with the Parmesan cheese and cook under the grill until browned. Serve at once, accompanied by sliced tomatoes, green salad and crusty bread.

serves 4 | prep 10 mins | cook 15 mins

cheesy baked courgettes

INGREDIENTS

4 courgettes

2 tbsp extra virgin olive oil

115 g/4 oz mozzarella cheese, thinly sliced

2 large tomatoes, deseeded and diced

**2 tsp fresh basil or oregano, chopped, plus extra
leaves to garnish**

Preheat the oven to 200°C/400°F/Gas Mark 6.
Slice the courgettes lengthways into 4 strips each.
Brush with oil and put in an ovenproof dish.

Bake the courgettes in the preheated oven for
10 minutes, or until softened but still holding
their shape.

Remove from the oven. Arrange the cheese slices
on top and sprinkle with the tomatoes and basil.
Return to the oven for 5 minutes, or until the
cheese has melted.

Carefully transfer the courgettes to serving plates,
or serve straight from the baking dish, garnished
with basil leaves.

serves 4 | prep 15 mins | cook 5–7 mins

classic stir-fried vegetables

INGREDIENTS
3 tbsp sesame oil
8 spring onions, finely chopped
1 garlic clove, crushed
1 tbsp grated fresh root ginger
1 head of broccoli, cut into florets
1 orange or yellow pepper, roughly chopped
125 g/4½ oz red cabbage, shredded
125 g/4½ oz baby sweetcorn
175 g/6 oz portobello or large cup mushrooms,
  thinly sliced
200 g/7 oz fresh beansprouts
250 g/9 oz canned water chestnuts,
  drained and rinsed
4 tsp soy sauce, or to taste
cooked mixed long-grain and wild rice, to serve

Heat 2 tablespoons of the oil in a preheated wok or large frying pan over a high heat. Add 6 of the spring onions, reserving the remainder for garnishing, the garlic and ginger and stir-fry for 30 seconds.

Add the broccoli, orange pepper and cabbage and stir-fry for 1–2 minutes. Add the sweetcorn and mushrooms and stir-fry for a further 1–2 minutes.

Finally, add the beansprouts and water chestnuts and stir-fry for a further 2 minutes. Add the soy sauce and stir well.

Transfer to warmed dishes and serve at once over cooked mixed long-grain and wild rice, garnished with the reserved spring onions.

serves 4–6 | prep 10 mins, plus 15 mins' standing | cook 15–30 mins

spanish tortilla

INGREDIENTS
125 ml/4 fl oz olive oil
600 g/1 lb 5 oz potatoes, peeled and thinly sliced
1 large onion, thinly sliced
6 large eggs
salt and pepper
fresh flat-leaf parsley sprigs, to garnish

Heat a 25-cm/10-inch frying pan, preferably non-stick, over a high heat. Add the oil and heat. Reduce the heat to medium–low, then add the potatoes and onion and cook, stirring occasionally, for 15–20 minutes until the potatoes are tender.

Beat the eggs in a large bowl and season generously with salt and pepper. Very gently stir the vegetables into the eggs. Set aside for 10 minutes. Drain the potatoes and onion through a sieve over a heatproof bowl to reserve the oil.

Use a wooden spoon or spatula to remove any crusty bits stuck to the base of the frying pan. Reheat the frying pan over a medium–high heat with 4 tablespoons of the reserved oil. Add the egg mixture and smooth the surface, pressing the potatoes and onions into an even layer.

Cook, shaking the pan occasionally, for 5 minutes, or until the bottom is set. Use a spatula to loosen the side of the tortilla. Put a large plate over the top and carefully invert the frying pan and plate together so that the tortilla drops onto the plate. Add 1 tablespoon of the remaining reserved oil to the frying pan and swirl around. Carefully slide the tortilla back into the pan, cooked-side up. Run the spatula around the tortilla, to tuck in the edge.

Cook for a further 3 minutes, or until the eggs are set and the bottom is golden brown. Remove from the heat and slide the tortilla onto a plate. Leave to stand for at least 5 minutes before cutting. Serve warm or at room temperature, garnished with parsley sprigs.

COOK'S TIP
If you are uncomfortable about inverting the tortilla, finish cooking it under a medium–high grill, about 10 cm/4 inches from the heat source, until the runny egg mixture on top is set. The tortilla will not, however, have its characteristic 'rounded' edge.

serves 4 | prep 15 mins | cook 15 mins

glazed vegetable kebabs

INGREDIENTS

150 ml/5 fl oz low-fat natural yogurt
4 tbsp mango chutney
1 tsp chopped garlic
1 tbsp lemon juice
8 baby onions, peeled but left whole
16 baby sweetcorn, halved
2 courgettes, cut into 2.5-cm/1-inch pieces
16 button mushrooms
16 cherry tomatoes
salt and pepper
mixed salad leaves, to garnish

Put the yogurt, chutney, garlic, lemon juice and salt and pepper to taste in a bowl, stir together and set aside.

Bring a saucepan of water to the boil, add the onions and return to the boil. Remove from the heat and drain well.

Thread the onions, sweetcorn, courgettes, mushrooms and tomatoes alternately onto 8 metal skewers or bamboo skewers presoaked in water for 30 minutes.

Preheat the grill to high. Arrange the kebabs on a grill rack and brush with the yogurt mixture. Cook under the grill, turning and brushing frequently with the remaining yogurt mixture, for 10 minutes, or until golden and tender.

Serve garnished with mixed salad leaves.

serves 4 | prep 15 mins | cook 20 mins

warm vegetable medley

INGREDIENTS
4 tbsp olive oil
2 celery sticks, sliced
2 red onions, sliced
450 g/1 lb aubergines, diced
1 garlic clove, finely chopped
5 plum tomatoes, chopped
3 tbsp red wine vinegar
1 tbsp sugar
3 tbsp green olives, stoned
2 tbsp capers
4 tbsp chopped fresh flat-leaf parsley
salt and pepper
hunks of fresh bread or rolls, to serve

Heat half the oil in a large, heavy-based saucepan over a low heat. Add the celery and onions and cook, stirring frequently, for 5 minutes, or until softened but not browned. Add the remaining oil and the aubergines and cook, stirring frequently, for 5 minutes, or until the aubergines begin to brown.

Add the garlic, tomatoes, vinegar and sugar and mix well. Cover the mixture with a round of greaseproof paper and simmer gently for 10 minutes.

Remove and discard the greaseproof paper, stir in the olives and capers and season to taste with salt and pepper. Tip the mixture into a serving dish and set aside to cool to room temperature. Sprinkle over the parsley and serve with hunks of bread or rolls.

COOK'S TIP
If possible, buy Sicilian capers for this dish. They are simply packed in salt and just need rinsing before use. Otherwise, use capers pickled in brine, but avoid those that are bottled in vinegar.

serves 4 | prep 15 mins | cook 5–8 mins

sweet-&-sour vegetables with cashew nuts

INGREDIENTS

1 tbsp vegetable or groundnut oil

1 tsp chilli oil

2 onions, sliced

2 carrots, thinly sliced

2 courgettes, thinly sliced

115 g/4 oz broccoli, cut into florets

115 g/4 oz button mushrooms, sliced

115 g/4 oz small pak choi, halved

2 tbsp palm sugar or soft light brown sugar

2 tbsp Thai soy sauce

1 tbsp rice vinegar

55 g/2 oz cashew nuts

Heat both the oils in a preheated wok or frying pan, add the onions and stir-fry for 1–2 minutes until beginning to soften.

Add the carrots, courgettes and broccoli and stir-fry for 2–3 minutes. Add the mushrooms, pak choi, sugar, soy sauce and vinegar and stir-fry for 1–2 minutes.

Meanwhile, heat a dry, heavy-based frying pan over a high heat, add the cashew nuts and cook, shaking the pan frequently, until lightly toasted. Sprinkle the cashew nuts over the stir-fry and serve at once.

serves 4 | prep 10 mins, plus 20 mins' marinating | cook 10 mins

spicy tofu

INGREDIENTS

MARINADE
5 tbsp vegetable stock
2 tsp cornflour
2 tbsp soy sauce
1 tbsp caster sugar
pinch of dried chilli flakes

STIR-FRY
250 g/9 oz firm tofu (drained weight),
  rinsed and drained thoroughly, then cut into
  1-cm/½-inch cubes
4 tbsp groundnut oil
1 tbsp grated fresh root ginger
3 garlic cloves, crushed
4 spring onions, thinly sliced
1 head of broccoli, cut into florets
1 carrot, cut into batons
1 yellow pepper, thinly sliced
250 g/9 oz shiitake mushrooms, thinly sliced
steamed rice, to serve

Blend all the marinade ingredients together in a large bowl. Add the tofu and toss well to coat. Cover and set aside to marinate for 20 minutes.

Heat half the oil in a preheated wok or large frying pan over a high heat, add the tofu with its marinade and stir-fry until browned and crisp. Remove from the wok and set aside.

Heat the remaining oil in the wok, add the ginger, garlic and spring onions and stir-fry for

30 seconds. Add the broccoli, carrot, yellow pepper and mushrooms and stir-fry for 5–6 minutes. Return the tofu to the wok and stir-fry to heat through.

Serve at once with steamed rice.

serves 4 | prep 10 mins | cook 6 mins

oyster mushrooms & vegetables with peanut chilli sauce

INGREDIENTS

1 tbsp sesame oil

4 spring onions, finely sliced

1 carrot, cut into batons

1 courgette, cut into batons

½ head of broccoli, cut into florets

450 g/1 lb oyster mushrooms, thinly sliced

2 tbsp crunchy peanut butter

1 tsp chilli powder, or to taste

3 tbsp water

lime wedges, to garnish

cooked rice or noodles, to serve

Heat the oil in a preheated wok or large frying pan until almost smoking, add the spring onions and stir-fry for 1 minute. Add the carrot and courgette and stir-fry for 1 minute. Add the broccoli and stir-fry for a further minute.

Add the mushrooms and stir-fry until softened and at least half the liquid they have produced has evaporated. Add the peanut butter and stir well, then add the chilli powder.

Finally, add the water and cook, stirring, for a further minute. Serve at once over cooked rice or noodles, garnished with lime wedges.

4

The following selection of main-course recipes shows just how varied vegetarian food can be. Here you will find definitive vegetarian versions of those perennially popular dishes – lasagne, moussaka, chilli and paella – along with that other crowd-pleasing standard, the nut loaf, featuring hazelnuts, carrots and coriander.

MAIN MEALS

Pasta fans are further catered for with a range of fresh vegetable and herb sauces, while rice lovers can feast on mouthwatering variations on the classic risotto theme. And curry enthusiasts have the pick of Thai- or Indian-style dishes, according to individual preference or mood. But for universal appeal and everyday satisfaction, a heart-warming stew is the easy winner.

serves 4 | prep 10 mins, plus 30 mins' standing | cook 45 mins

ratatouille with baked jacket potatoes

INGREDIENTS
1 aubergine, about 250 g/9 oz
4 tbsp olive oil
2 garlic cloves, chopped
1 large onion, chopped
2 red peppers, deseeded and cut into
  bite-sized chunks
800 g/1 lb 12 oz canned chopped tomatoes
2 courgettes, sliced
1 celery stick, sliced
1 tsp sugar
salt and pepper
2 tbsp chopped fresh thyme, plus extra sprigs
  to garnish

TO SERVE
freshly baked jacket potatoes with butter
fresh crusty bread

Trim the aubergine, cut it into bite-sized chunks and put in a colander. Sprinkle with salt and leave to stand for about 30 minutes.

Heat the oil in a large saucepan over a medium heat. Add the garlic and onion and cook, stirring frequently, for 3 minutes, or until slightly softened. Rinse the aubergine and drain well, then add it to the saucepan with the peppers. Reduce the heat and cook gently, stirring occasionally, for a further 10 minutes.

Stir in the tomatoes, courgettes, celery, sugar and chopped thyme and season to taste with salt and pepper. Bring to the boil, then reduce the heat, cover and simmer gently for 30 minutes.

Remove from the heat, transfer to serving plates and garnish with thyme sprigs. Serve with buttered hot jacket potatoes and crusty bread.

serves 4 | prep 10 mins, plus 30 mins' standing | cook 1¼ hrs

imam bayildi

INGREDIENTS

2 aubergines, about 275 g/9½ oz each
6 tbsp olive oil
3 garlic cloves, chopped
2 onions, chopped
750 g/1 lb 10 oz canned chopped tomatoes
2 red peppers, deseeded and chopped
1 celery stick, sliced
1 tbsp raisins
1 tbsp sultanas
pinch of freshly grated nutmeg
salt and pepper
1 tbsp chopped fresh flat-leaf parsley, plus extra
  sprigs to garnish
freshly cooked rice, to serve

Cut each aubergine in half lengthways. Scoop out the flesh, leaving 1 cm/½ inch of flesh around the inside of each shell. Chop the flesh. Sprinkle the flesh and shells with salt and leave to stand for 30 minutes.

Preheat the oven to 180°C/350°F/Gas Mark 4. Heat half the oil in a saucepan over a medium heat. Add the garlic and onion and cook, stirring frequently, for 3 minutes, or until slightly softened. Rinse the aubergine and drain well, then add the flesh to the saucepan with the tomatoes. Cook, stirring frequently, for 10 minutes. Add the red peppers, celery, raisins, sultanas, nutmeg and chopped parsley to the saucepan and season to taste with salt and pepper. Reduce the heat, cover and simmer for 15 minutes.

Put the aubergine shells in an ovenproof dish. Spoon the tomato mixture into the shells. Drizzle with the remaining oil, cover with foil and bake in the preheated oven for 45 minutes. Remove from the oven and leave to cool to room temperature. Garnish with parsley sprigs and serve with freshly cooked rice. Alternatively, to serve cold, leave the aubergines to cool completely, cover with clingfilm and chill in the refrigerator until required. Remove from the refrigerator 1 hour before serving.

serves 4 | prep 20 mins | cook 40–45 mins

cannelloni with spinach & ricotta

INGREDIENTS
12 dried cannelloni tubes, 7.5 cm/3 inches long
butter, for greasing

FILLING
140 g/5 oz frozen spinach, thawed and drained
115 g/4 oz ricotta cheese
1 egg
3 tbsp freshly grated pecorino cheese
pinch of freshly grated nutmeg
salt and pepper

CHEESE SAUCE
600 ml/1 pint milk
25 g/1 oz unsalted butter
2 tbsp plain flour
85 g/3 oz freshly grated Gruyère cheese
salt and pepper

Bring a large saucepan of lightly salted water to the boil. Add the cannelloni tubes, return to the boil and cook for 6–7 minutes until almost tender. Drain, refresh under cold running water and drain again. Spread out the tubes on a clean tea towel.

Put the spinach and ricotta in a blender or food processor and process for a few seconds until combined. Add the egg and pecorino cheese and process again to a smooth paste. Scrape the filling into a bowl and season to taste with nutmeg and salt and pepper.

Preheat the oven to 180°C/350°F/Gas Mark 4. Grease an ovenproof dish. Spoon the filling into a piping bag fitted with a 1-cm/½-inch nozzle. Open

a cannelloni tube, stand it upright and pipe in the filling. Put the filled cannelloni tube in the prepared dish, then fill the remaining cannelloni tubes.

To make the cheese sauce, heat the milk in a saucepan to just below boiling point. Meanwhile, melt the butter in a separate saucepan over a low heat. Add the flour to the butter and cook, stirring constantly, for 1 minute. Remove from the heat and gradually stir in the hot milk. Return to the heat and bring to the boil, stirring constantly. Reduce the heat to the lowest possible setting and simmer, stirring frequently, for 10 minutes, or until thickened and smooth. Remove from the heat, stir in the Gruyère cheese and season to taste with salt and pepper.

Spoon the cheese sauce over the filled cannelloni. Cover the dish with foil and bake in the preheated oven for 20–25 minutes. Serve at once.

serves 4 | prep 10 mins | cook 25 mins

fusilli with courgette, lemon & rosemary sauce

INGREDIENTS
6 tbsp olive oil
1 small onion, very thinly sliced
2 garlic cloves, very finely chopped
2 tbsp chopped fresh rosemary
1 tbsp chopped fresh flat-leaf parsley
450 g/1 lb small courgettes, cut into
    4-cm-x-5-mm/1½-x-¼-inch strips
finely grated rind of 1 lemon
450 g/1 lb dried fusilli
4 tbsp freshly grated Parmesan cheese
salt and pepper

Heat the oil in a large frying pan over a medium–low heat. Add the onion and cook, stirring occasionally, for 10 minutes, or until golden.

Increase the heat to medium–high. Add the garlic, rosemary and parsley and cook, stirring, for a few seconds.

Add the courgettes and lemon rind and cook, stirring occasionally, for 5–7 minutes until the courgettes are just tender. Season to taste with salt and pepper. Remove from the heat.

Meanwhile, bring a large saucepan of salted water to the boil. Add the pasta, return to the boil and cook for 8–10 minutes until tender but still firm to the bite. Drain the pasta and transfer to a warmed serving dish.

Briefly reheat the courgette sauce. Pour over the pasta and toss well to mix. Sprinkle with the Parmesan cheese and serve at once.

pasta all'arrabbiata

INGREDIENTS
150 ml/5 fl oz dry white wine
1 tbsp sun-dried tomato paste
2 fresh red chillies
2 garlic cloves, finely chopped
350 g/12 oz dried tortiglioni
4 tbsp chopped fresh flat-leaf parsley
salt and pepper
fresh pecorino cheese shavings, to garnish

SUGOCASA
5 tbsp extra virgin olive oil
450 g/1 lb plum tomatoes, chopped
salt and pepper

First make the sugocasa. Heat the oil in a frying pan over a high heat until almost smoking. Add the tomatoes and cook, stirring frequently, for 2–3 minutes. Reduce the heat to low and cook gently for 20 minutes, or until very soft. Season to taste with salt and pepper. Press through a non-metallic sieve with a wooden spoon into a saucepan.

Add the wine, tomato paste, whole chillies and garlic to the sugocasa and bring to the boil. Reduce the heat and simmer gently.

Meanwhile, bring a large saucepan of lightly salted water to the boil. Add the pasta, return to the boil and cook for 8–10 minutes until tender but still firm to the bite.

Remove the chillies and taste the sauce. If you prefer a hotter flavour, chop some or all of the chillies and return to the saucepan. Check and adjust the seasoning, if necessary, then stir in half the parsley.

Drain the pasta and transfer to a warmed serving bowl. Add the sauce and toss to coat. Sprinkle with the remaining parsley, garnish with the pecorino cheese shavings and serve at once.

COOK'S TIP
If time is short, use ready-made sugocasa, available from most supermarkets and sometimes labelled 'crushed tomatoes'. Failing that, you could use passata, but the sauce will be thinner.

serves 4 | prep 10 mins | cook 20 mins

chilli broccoli pasta

INGREDIENTS
225 g/8 oz dried penne or macaroni
225 g/8 oz broccoli, cut into florets
50 ml/2 fl oz extra virgin olive oil
2 large garlic cloves, chopped
2 fresh red chillies, deseeded and diced
8 cherry tomatoes (optional)
fresh basil leaves, to garnish

Bring a large saucepan of salted boiling water to
the boil. Add the pasta, return to the boil and cook
for 8–10 minutes until tender but still firm to the
bite. Drain the pasta, refresh under cold running
water and drain again. Set aside.

Bring a separate saucepan of salted water to the
boil, add the broccoli and cook for 5 minutes.
Drain, refresh under cold running water and
drain again.

Heat the oil in the saucepan that the pasta was
cooked in over a high heat. Add the garlic, chillies
and tomatoes, if using, and cook, stirring, for
1 minute.

Add the broccoli and mix well. Cook for 2 minutes,
stirring, to heat through. Add the pasta and mix
well again. Cook for a further minute. Transfer the
pasta to a large, warmed serving bowl and serve
garnished with basil leaves.

serves 4 | prep 10 mins, plus 30 mins' standing | cook 8–10 mins

conchiglie with raw tomato, garlic & basil sauce

INGREDIENTS
**550 g/1 lb 4 oz large, ripe tomatoes, peeled,
  deseeded and diced**
125 ml/4 fl oz extra virgin olive oil
4 garlic cloves, very finely chopped
large handful of fresh basil leaves, shredded
3 tbsp chopped fresh oregano or marjoram
450 g/1 lb dried conchiglie
salt and pepper

Combine the tomatoes, oil, garlic, basil and
oregano in a bowl that is large enough to
accommodate the cooked pasta. Season
generously with salt and pepper. Cover the
bowl with clingfilm and leave to stand at room
temperature for at least 30 minutes.

Bring a large saucepan of salted water to the boil.
Add the pasta, return to the boil and cook for
8–10 minutes until tender but still firm to the bite.
Drain thoroughly and immediately add to the
tomato mixture.

Toss well to mix. Serve at room temperature.

serves 4 | prep 5 mins | cook 30 mins

basic risotto

INGREDIENTS

2 litres/3½ pints vegetable stock or water
3 tbsp butter
1 tbsp olive oil
1 small onion, finely chopped
450 g/1 lb arborio rice
salt and pepper
55 g/2 oz freshly grated Parmesan or
  Grana Padano cheese, plus extra shavings
  to garnish

Bring the stock to the boil in a saucepan, then reduce the heat and keep simmering gently over a low heat while you are cooking the risotto.

Melt 2 tablespoons of the butter with the oil in a deep saucepan over a medium heat. Add the onion and cook, stirring frequently, for 5 minutes, or until softened but not browned.

Add the rice, stir to coat in the butter and oil and cook, stirring constantly, for 2–3 minutes until the grains are translucent. Gradually add the hot stock, a ladle at a time, stirring constantly and adding more liquid as the rice absorbs it. Cook for 20 minutes, or until all the liquid is absorbed and the risotto is creamy but still with a little bite to the rice. Season to taste with salt and pepper, but bear in mind that the Parmesan cheese is salty.

Remove from the heat and add the remaining butter. Mix well, then stir in the Parmesan cheese until it has melted. Taste and adjust the seasoning, if necessary, and serve at once, garnished with Parmesan cheese shavings.

serves 4 | prep 5 mins | cook 30 mins

red wine, herb &
sun-dried tomato risotto

INGREDIENTS

1 quantity basic risotto made with half vegetable
  stock, half strong Italian red wine
6 sun-dried tomatoes in olive oil, drained and
  finely chopped
1 tbsp chopped fresh thyme, plus extra sprigs
  to garnish
1 tbsp chopped fresh parsley
10–12 fresh basil leaves, shredded, to garnish

Prepare the basic risotto, folding in the sun-dried
tomatoes after the first addition of stock-wine
mixture has been absorbed.

Carefully fold the herbs into the risotto 5 minutes
before the end of cooking time.

Serve the risotto garnished with the shredded
basil leaves and thyme sprigs.

serves 4 | prep 5 mins | cook 30 mins

risotto with roasted vegetables

INGREDIENTS

1 quantity basic risotto, made with vegetable
  stock or half stock and half dry white wine
225 g/8 oz roasted vegetables, such as peppers,
  courgettes and aubergines, cut into chunks
2 tbsp fresh herbs, finely chopped, to garnish

Prepare the basic risotto, adding most of the
roasted vegetables to the risotto 5 minutes before
the end of cooking time to heat through. Reserve
a few large pieces for garnishing.

Spoon the risotto onto individual warmed plates,
arrange the reserved vegetables around it or on
top to garnish, then scatter with fresh herbs
before serving at once.

vegetable paella

INGREDIENTS
¼ tsp saffron threads
3 tbsp hot water
6 tbsp olive oil
1 Spanish onion, sliced
3 garlic cloves, finely chopped
1 red pepper, deseeded and sliced
1 orange pepper, deseeded and sliced
1 large aubergine, cut into cubes
225 g/8 oz risotto rice
600 ml/1 pint vegetable stock
450 g/1 lb tomatoes, peeled and chopped
115 g/4 oz mushrooms, sliced
115 g/4 oz French beans, halved
400 g/14 oz canned pinto beans
salt and pepper

Put the saffron and water in a bowl and set aside. Meanwhile, heat the oil in a large frying pan or paella pan over a medium heat. Add the onion and cook, stirring frequently, for 5 minutes, or until softened. Add the garlic, peppers and aubergine and cook, stirring occasionally, for 5 minutes.

Add the rice and cook, stirring constantly, for 1 minute, or until the grains are well coated in oil.

Stir in the stock, tomatoes and saffron and its soaking liquid and season to taste with salt and pepper. Bring to the boil, then reduce the heat and simmer, shaking the frying pan frequently and stirring occasionally, for 15 minutes.

Stir in the mushrooms, French beans and pinto beans with their can juices. Cook for a further 10 minutes, stirring occasionally. Serve at once.

serves 4 | prep 30 mins | cook 15 mins

lentil & rice pilaf
with celery, carrots & orange

INGREDIENTS

4 tbsp vegetable oil

1 red onion, finely chopped

2 tender celery sticks, leaves included,
   quartered lengthways and diced

2 carrots, coarsely grated

1 fresh green chilli, deseeded and finely chopped

3 spring onions, green parts included, finely
   chopped

40 g/1½ oz whole blanched almonds,
   sliced lengthways

350 g/12 oz cooked brown basmati rice

150 g/5½ oz cooked red split lentils

175 ml/6 fl oz vegetable stock

5 tbsp fresh orange juice

salt and pepper

Heat half the oil in a high-sided frying pan with a lid over a medium heat. Add the onion and cook, stirring frequently, for 5 minutes, or until softened.

Add the celery, carrots, chilli, spring onions and almonds. Stir-fry for 2 minutes, or until the vegetables are al dente but still brightly coloured. Transfer to a bowl and set aside.

Add the remaining oil to the pan over a medium–high heat. Add the rice and lentils and cook, stirring, for 1–2 minutes until heated through. Reduce the heat and stir in the stock and orange juice. Season to taste with salt and pepper.

Return the vegetables to the pan. Toss with the rice for a few minutes until heated through. Transfer to a warmed serving dish and serve at once.

serves 4 | prep 10 mins | cook 1½ hrs

caribbean rice & peas

INGREDIENTS

115 g/4 oz dried gunga peas, soaked overnight in water to cover
225 g/8 oz long-grain rice
700 ml/1¼ pints water
55 g/2 oz creamed coconut
1 onion, chopped
2 garlic cloves, finely chopped
1 small red pepper, deseeded and chopped
1 tbsp fresh thyme leaves
1 bay leaf
½ tsp ground mixed spice
salt and pepper

COOK'S TIP

Gunga peas go by a variety of names, including pigeon, Congo and Jamaica peas. Fresh gunga peas, sometimes known as Cajun peas, also feature in Caribbean cooking.

Drain the gunga peas and put in a large saucepan. Add enough cold water to cover by about 2.5 cm/ 1 inch. Bring to the boil, then reduce the heat and simmer for 1 hour, or until tender. Drain and return to the saucepan.

Add the rice, water, coconut, onion, garlic, red pepper, thyme, bay leaf and mixed spice and season to taste with salt and pepper. Bring to the boil, stirring constantly, and boil until the creamed coconut has melted, then reduce the heat, cover and simmer for 20 minutes.

Uncover the saucepan and cook the rice mixture for a further 5 minutes, or until any excess liquid has evaporated. Fork through the rice to fluff up the grains, then serve at once.

serves 4 | prep 15 mins, plus 30 mins' standing | cook 1 hr

vegetable polenta

INGREDIENTS

1 aubergine, about 250 g/9 oz, sliced

300 g/10½ oz polenta

1.2 litres/2 pints vegetable stock

6 tbsp olive oil, plus extra for oiling

1 garlic clove, chopped

2 red onions, sliced

850 g/1 lb 14 oz small new potatoes, halved

1 red pepper, deseeded and cut into strips

1 orange pepper, deseeded and cut into strips

2 courgettes, sliced

3 tbsp sun-dried tomatoes in olive oil,
   drained and chopped

1 tbsp chopped fresh rosemary

salt and pepper

1 tbsp chopped fresh flat-leaf parsley,
   plus extra sprigs to garnish

Put the aubergine slices in a colander. Sprinkle with salt and leave to stand for 30 minutes.

Preheat the oven to 190°C/375°F/Gas Mark 5. Oil an ovenproof dish.

Put the polenta and stock in a large saucepan and bring to the boil, stirring constantly. Boil for 10 minutes, stirring, then transfer to the oiled dish. Bake in the preheated oven for 45 minutes, turning the polenta over halfway through the cooking time.

Meanwhile, heat half the oil in a large saucepan over a medium heat. Add the garlic and onions and cook, stirring frequently, for 3 minutes. Rinse the aubergine, drain well and pat dry. Add to the saucepan with the potatoes, peppers, courgettes, tomatoes, rosemary and parsley. Season to taste with salt and pepper. Cook, stirring frequently, for 5 minutes, then reduce the heat and cook, stirring occasionally, for 10 minutes.

Lightly oil a baking tray and spread the vegetables out on it. Drizzle over the remaining oil, then roast in the oven for 20 minutes, turning over halfway through the cooking time. To serve, cut the polenta into wedges and arrange with the roasted vegetables on serving plates, garnished with parsley sprigs.

serves 4 | prep 15 mins | cook 20 mins

thai green curry

INGREDIENTS
150 g/5½ oz broccoli florets
150 g/5½ oz mangetout
2 tbsp chilli oil
350 ml/12 fl oz canned coconut milk
200 g/7 oz firm marinated tofu, cut into cubes
1 green pepper, deseeded and sliced
1 yellow pepper, deseeded and sliced
1 tbsp soy sauce
100 g/3½ oz beansprouts
1 tbsp chopped fresh coriander, plus extra
  sprigs to garnish
salt and pepper
freshly cooked noodles, to serve

GREEN CURRY PASTE
8 fresh green chillies, chopped
2 tbsp chopped spring onions
2 tsp chopped fresh kaffir lime leaves
2 large garlic cloves, finely chopped
2.5-cm/1-inch piece fresh root ginger, grated
1 tbsp finely chopped fresh lemon grass
2 tsp ground coriander
½ tsp ground cumin
½ tsp salt
2 tbsp chilli oil

To make the green curry paste, put all the ingredients in a food processor and process until smooth. Transfer to a bowl, cover with clingfilm and refrigerate until required. Bring a large saucepan of water to the boil, add the broccoli and mangetout and cook for 2 minutes. Drain, refresh under cold running water, then drain again.

Heat the oil in a large saucepan over a medium heat, add 2 tablespoons of the curry paste and cook, stirring, for 1 minute. Stir in 4 tablespoons of the coconut milk, then add the tofu, broccoli, mangetout, peppers and soy sauce. Cook for 5 minutes, then stir in the remaining coconut milk and bring to the boil. Reduce the heat, add the beansprouts and cook for a further 5 minutes. Stir in the chopped coriander, season to taste with salt and pepper and heat through.

Spoon over freshly cooked noodles, garnish with coriander sprigs and serve at once.

serves 4 | prep 20 mins | cook 40–50 mins

vegetable & coconut curry

INGREDIENTS
1 onion, roughly chopped
3 garlic cloves, thinly sliced
2.5-cm/1-inch piece fresh root ginger, thinly sliced
2 fresh green chillies, deseeded and
 finely chopped
1 tbsp vegetable oil
1 tsp ground turmeric
1 tsp ground coriander
1 tsp ground cumin
1 kg/2 lb 4 oz mixed vegetables, such as
cauliflower, courgettes, potatoes, carrots and
 French beans, cut into chunks
200 g/7 oz creamed coconut
600 ml/1 pint boiling water
salt and pepper
2 tbsp chopped fresh coriander, to garnish
freshly cooked rice, to serve

Put the onion, garlic, ginger and chillies in a food processor and process until almost smooth.

Heat the oil in a large, heavy-based saucepan over a medium–low heat, add the onion mixture and cook, stirring constantly, for 5 minutes.

Add the turmeric, ground coriander and cumin and cook, stirring frequently, for 3–4 minutes. Add the vegetables and stir to coat in the spice paste.

Mix the creamed coconut and boiling water together in a heatproof jug and stir until dissolved. Add the coconut mixture to the vegetables, cover and simmer for 30–40 minutes until the vegetables are tender.

Season to taste with salt and pepper, garnish with the chopped fresh coriander and serve with rice.

serves 4 | prep 20 mins | cook 45 mins

mixed vegetable curry

INGREDIENTS

1 aubergine
225 g/8 oz turnips
350 g/12 oz new potatoes
225 g/8 oz cauliflower
225 g/8 oz button mushrooms
1 large onion
3 carrots
6 tbsp ghee or vegetable oil
2 garlic cloves, crushed
4 tsp finely chopped fresh root ginger
1–2 fresh green chillies, deseeded and chopped
1 tbsp paprika
2 tsp ground coriander
1 tbsp mild or medium curry powder
450 ml/16 fl oz vegetable stock
400 g/14 oz canned chopped tomatoes
1 green pepper, deseeded and sliced
1 tbsp cornflour
150 ml/5 fl oz coconut milk
2–3 tbsp ground almonds
salt
fresh coriander sprigs, to garnish
freshly cooked rice, to serve

Cut the aubergine, turnips and potatoes into
1-cm/½-inch cubes. Break the cauliflower into
small florets. Leave the mushrooms whole if small
or slice them thickly, if preferred. Slice the onion
and carrots.

Heat the ghee in a large saucepan over a low
heat. Add the onion, turnips, potatoes and
cauliflower and cook, stirring frequently, for
3 minutes.

Add the garlic, ginger, chilli, paprika, ground
coriander and curry powder and cook, stirring
constantly, for 1 minute.

Add the stock, tomatoes, aubergine and
mushrooms and season to taste with salt. Cover
and simmer, stirring occasionally, for 30 minutes,
or until tender. Add the green pepper and carrots,
cover and cook for a further 5 minutes.

Put the cornflour and coconut milk in a bowl, mix
into a smooth paste and stir into the vegetable
mixture. Add the ground almonds and simmer,
stirring constantly, for 2 minutes. Taste and adjust
the seasoning, if necessary. Transfer to serving
plates, garnish with coriander sprigs and serve at
once with freshly cooked rice.

serves 4 | prep 20 mins | cook 40 mins

vegetable korma

INGREDIENTS
4 tbsp ghee or vegetable oil
2 onions, chopped
2 garlic cloves, chopped
1 fresh red chilli, chopped
1 tbsp grated fresh root ginger
2 tomatoes, peeled and chopped
1 orange pepper, deseeded and cut into
  small pieces
1 large potato, cut into chunks
200 g/7 oz cauliflower florets
½ tsp salt
1 tsp turmeric
1 tsp ground cumin
1 tsp ground coriander
1 tsp garam masala
200 ml/7 fl oz vegetable stock or water
150 ml/5 fl oz natural yogurt
150 ml/5 fl oz single cream
25 g/1 oz fresh coriander, chopped
freshly cooked rice, to serve

Heat the ghee in a large saucepan over a medium heat, add the onions and garlic and cook, stirring frequently, for 3 minutes. Add the chilli and ginger and cook for a further 4 minutes. Add the tomatoes, orange pepper, potato, cauliflower, salt and spices and cook, stirring constantly, for a further 3 minutes. Stir in the stock and bring to the boil. Reduce the heat and simmer for 25 minutes.

Stir in the yogurt and cream and cook, stirring frequently, for a further 5 minutes without boiling. Add the fresh coriander and heat through.

Serve with freshly cooked rice.

serves 4 | prep 15 mins, plus 1 hr chilling | cook 12–15 mins

spinach & ricotta dumplings

INGREDIENTS

1 kg/2 lb 4 oz fresh spinach leaves,
  tough stalks removed
350 g/12 oz ricotta cheese
115 g/4 oz freshly grated Parmesan cheese
3 eggs, lightly beaten
pinch of freshly grated nutmeg
115–175 g/4–6 oz plain flour, plus extra
  for dusting
salt and pepper

HERB BUTTER

115 g/4 oz unsalted butter
2 tbsp chopped fresh oregano
2 tbsp chopped fresh sage

Wash the spinach, then put in a saucepan with just the water clinging to its leaves. Cover and cook over a low heat for 6–8 minutes until just wilted. Drain well and leave to cool.

Squeeze or press out as much liquid as possible from the spinach, then finely chop or process in a food processor. Put the spinach in a bowl and add the ricotta, half the Parmesan cheese, the eggs, nutmeg and salt and pepper to taste. Beat until thoroughly combined. Sift in 115 g/4 oz of the flour and lightly work it into the mixture, adding more, if necessary, to make a workable mixture. Cover with clingfilm and chill in the refrigerator for 1 hour.

With floured hands, break off small pieces of the mixture and roll into walnut-sized balls.

Handle them as little as possible, as they are quite delicate. Lightly dust the dumplings with flour.

Bring a large saucepan of lightly salted water to the boil. Add the dumplings and cook for 2–3 minutes until they rise to the surface. Remove with a slotted spoon, drain well and set aside.

Meanwhile, make the herb butter. Melt the butter in a large, heavy-based frying pan over a low heat. Add the oregano and sage and cook, stirring frequently, for 1 minute. Add the dumplings and toss gently for 1 minute to coat. Transfer to a warmed serving dish, sprinkle with the remaining Parmesan cheese and serve at once.

serves 4 | prep 20 mins, plus 10 mins' cooling | cook 1¼ hrs

vegetable & hazelnut loaf

INGREDIENTS

2 tbsp sunflower oil, plus extra for oiling
1 onion, chopped
1 garlic clove, finely chopped
2 celery sticks, chopped
1 tbsp plain flour
200 ml/7 fl oz passata
115 g/4 oz fresh wholemeal breadcrumbs
2 carrots, grated
115 g/4 oz toasted hazelnuts, ground
1 tbsp dark soy sauce
2 tbsp chopped fresh coriander
1 egg, lightly beaten
salt and pepper

Put the breadcrumbs, carrots, ground hazelnuts, soy sauce and coriander in a bowl. Add the tomato mixture and stir well. Leave to cool slightly, then beat in the egg and season to taste with salt and pepper.

Spoon the mixture into the prepared tin and smooth the surface. Cover with foil and bake in the preheated oven for 1 hour. If serving hot, turn the loaf out onto a warmed serving dish and serve at once. Alternatively, leave to cool in the tin before turning out.

Preheat the oven to 180°C/350°F/Gas Mark 4. Oil and line a 450-g/1-lb loaf tin. Heat the oil in a heavy-based frying pan over a medium heat. Add the onion and cook, stirring frequently, for 5 minutes, or until softened. Add the garlic and celery and cook, stirring frequently, for 5 minutes. Add the flour and cook, stirring constantly, for 1 minute. Gradually stir in the passata and cook, stirring constantly, until thickened. Remove the pan from the heat.

VARIATION

You can cook the loaf in a round cake tin and serve in wedges for a different presentation, if desired.

serves 4 | prep 10 mins | cook 45 mins

cauliflower bake

INGREDIENTS
500 g/1 lb 2 oz cauliflower, broken into florets
600 g/1 lb 5 oz potatoes, cut into cubes
100 g/3½ oz cherry tomatoes

SAUCE
25 g/1 oz butter or margarine
1 leek, sliced
1 garlic clove, crushed
3 tbsp plain flour
300 ml/10 fl oz milk
85 g/3 oz mixed cheese, such as Cheddar,
  Parmesan and Gruyère, grated
½ tsp paprika
2 tbsp chopped fresh flat-leaf parsley,
  plus extra to garnish
salt and pepper

Preheat the oven to 180°C/350°F/Gas Mark 4. Bring a large saucepan of salted water to the boil, add the cauliflower and cook for 10 minutes. Meanwhile, bring a separate large saucepan of salted water to the boil, add the potatoes and cook for 10 minutes. Drain both vegetables and set aside.

To make the sauce, melt the butter in a large saucepan, add the leek and garlic and cook over a low heat for 1 minute. Stir in the flour and cook, stirring constantly, for 1 minute. Remove from the heat, then gradually stir in the milk, 55 g/2 oz of the cheese, the paprika and parsley. Return to the heat and bring to the boil, stirring constantly. Season to taste with salt and pepper.

Transfer the cauliflower to a deep, ovenproof dish with the tomatoes and top with the potatoes. Pour the sauce over the potatoes and sprinkle over the remaining cheese.

Cook in the preheated oven for 20 minutes, or until the vegetables are cooked through and the cheese is golden brown and bubbling. Garnish with chopped parsley and serve at once.

VARIATION
You can use broccoli instead of cauliflower for this dish, if you prefer. Alternatively, use a mixture of broccoli and cauliflower for a combination of colours.

serves 4–6 | prep 10 mins | cook 1 hr 5 mins

tomato & onion bake with eggs

INGREDIENTS
55 g/2 oz butter, plus extra for greasing
2 large onions, thinly sliced
500 g/1 lb 2 oz tomatoes, peeled and sliced
115 g/4 oz fresh white breadcrumbs
4 eggs
salt and pepper

Preheat the oven to 180°C/350°F/Gas Mark 4. Grease an ovenproof dish.

Melt 3 tablespoons of the butter in a heavy-based frying pan over a low heat. Add the onions and cook, stirring frequently, for 5 minutes, or until softened.

Layer the onions, tomatoes and breadcrumbs in the prepared dish, seasoning each layer with salt and pepper to taste. Dot the remaining butter on top. Bake in the preheated oven for 40 minutes.

Remove the bake from the oven and make 4 hollows in the mixture with the back of a spoon. Crack 1 egg into each hollow. Return the dish to the oven for a further 15 minutes, or until the eggs are just set. Serve at once.

VARIATION
For added spice, deseed and slice 2 red peppers and add once the onions have softened. Cook for 10 minutes, then stir in a pinch of cayenne pepper.

serves 4 | prep 15 mins | cook 40 mins

vegetable crumble

INGREDIENTS
1 cauliflower, cut into florets
2 tbsp sunflower oil
25 g/1 oz plain flour
350 ml/12 fl oz milk
325 g/11½ oz canned sweetcorn kernels, drained
2 tbsp chopped fresh parsley
1 tsp chopped fresh thyme
140 g/5 oz Cheddar cheese, grated
salt and pepper

TOPPING
55 g/2 oz wholemeal flour
25 g/1 oz butter
25 g/1 oz rolled oats
25 g/1 oz blanched almonds, chopped

Preheat the oven to 190°C/375°F/Gas Mark 5. Bring a large saucepan of lightly salted water to the boil, add the cauliflower and cook for 5 minutes. Drain well, reserving the cooking liquid. Heat the oil in a saucepan over a medium heat and stir in the flour. Cook, stirring constantly, for 1 minute. Remove from the heat and gradually stir in the milk and 150 ml/5 fl oz of the reserved cooking liquid. Return to the heat and bring to the boil, stirring constantly. Cook, stirring, for 3 minutes, or until thickened. Remove from the heat.

Stir the sweetcorn, parsley, thyme and half the cheese into the sauce and season to taste with salt and pepper. Fold in the cauliflower, then spoon the mixture into an ovenproof dish.

To make the crumble topping, put the flour in a bowl, add the butter and rub into the flour with your fingertips until the mixture resembles breadcrumbs. Stir in the oats and almonds, add the remaining cheese, then sprinkle the mixture evenly over the vegetables. Bake in the preheated oven for 30 minutes. Serve at once.

VARIATION
For extra colour, replace half the cauliflower with fresh green broccoli at the beginning of the recipe.

serves 4–6 | prep 20 mins, plus 10 mins' standing | cook 45 mins

mixed vegetable stew

INGREDIENTS

about 125 ml/4 fl oz olive oil
2 large onions, thinly sliced
4 large garlic cloves, crushed
300 g/10½ oz aubergine, cut into 1-cm/½-inch cubes
300 g/10½ oz yellow or green courgettes, cut into 1-cm/½-inch cubes
1 large red pepper, deseeded and chopped
1 large yellow pepper, deseeded and chopped
1 large green pepper, deseeded and chopped
2 fresh thyme sprigs
1 bay leaf
1 small young fresh rosemary sprig
100 ml/3½ fl oz vegetable stock
450 g/1 lb large, juicy tomatoes, peeled, deseeded and chopped
salt and pepper
fresh basil or oregano sprigs, to garnish

Heat about 2 tablespoons of the oil in a large, flameproof casserole over a medium heat. Add the onions and cook, stirring frequently, for 5 minutes, or until softened but not browned. Add the garlic and cook, stirring, for 1 minute. Reduce the heat to very low.

Meanwhile, heat a frying pan over a high heat until you can feel the heat rising. Add 1 tablespoon of the remaining oil and the aubergine cubes to make a single layer. Cook, stirring, until slightly brown on all sides. Transfer to the casserole with the onions.

Heat a further tablespoon of the remaining oil in the frying pan. Add the courgettes and cook,

stirring, until lightly browned all over. Transfer to the casserole. Heat another tablespoon of the remaining oil in the pan, add the peppers and cook, stirring, until softened. Transfer to the casserole.

Stir the thyme, bay leaf, rosemary, stock and salt and pepper to taste into the casserole and bring to the boil. Reduce the heat to very low, cover and simmer, stirring occasionally, for 20 minutes, or until the vegetables are tender and blended.

Remove from the heat and stir in the tomatoes. Cover and set aside for 10 minutes for the tomatoes to soften. Serve, or leave to cool completely and then serve chilled the next day, garnished with basil or oregano sprigs.

serves 4 | prep 15 mins | cook 2¼–2½ hrs

provençal bean stew

INGREDIENTS

350 g/12 oz dried pinto beans,
  soaked overnight in water to cover
2 tbsp olive oil
2 onions, sliced
2 garlic cloves, finely chopped
1 red pepper, deseeded and sliced
1 yellow pepper, deseeded and sliced
400 g/14 oz canned chopped tomatoes
2 tbsp tomato purée
1 tbsp torn fresh basil leaves
2 tsp chopped fresh thyme
2 tsp chopped fresh rosemary
1 bay leaf
55 g/2 oz black olives, stoned and halved
salt and pepper
2 tbsp chopped fresh parsley, to garnish

Drain the beans. Place in a large saucepan, add enough cold water to cover and bring to the boil. Reduce the heat, then cover and simmer for 1¼–1½ hours until almost tender. Drain, reserving 300 ml/10 fl oz of the cooking liquid.

Heat the oil in a heavy-based saucepan over a medium heat. Add the onions and cook, stirring frequently, for 5 minutes, or until softened. Add the garlic and peppers and cook, stirring occasionally, for 10 minutes.

Add the tomatoes and their can juices, the remaining reserved cooking liquid, tomato purée, basil, thyme, rosemary, bay leaf and beans. Season to taste with salt and pepper. Cover and simmer for 40 minutes. Add the olives and simmer for a further 5 minutes. Transfer to a warmed serving dish, sprinkle with the parsley and serve at once.

COOK'S TIP

When using beans, always follow the packet instructions for soaking and cooking. If you use borlotti or red kidney beans, boil them vigorously for 15 minutes before simmering.

serves 4 | prep 20 mins | cook 1¼ hrs

vegetable chilli

INGREDIENTS

1 aubergine, cut into 2.5-cm/1-inch slices
1 tbsp olive oil, plus extra for brushing
1 large red or yellow onion, finely chopped
2 red or yellow peppers, deseeded
   and finely chopped
3–4 garlic cloves, finely chopped or crushed
800 g/1 lb 12 oz canned chopped tomatoes
1 tbsp mild chilli powder
½ tsp ground cumin
½ tsp dried oregano
2 small courgettes, quartered lengthways
   and sliced
400 g/14 oz canned kidney beans, drained
   and rinsed
450 ml/16 fl oz water
1 tbsp tomato purée
6 spring onions, finely chopped
115 g/4 oz Cheddar cheese, grated
salt and pepper

Brush the aubergine slices on one side with oil.
Heat half the oil in a large, heavy-based frying pan
over a medium heat. Add the aubergine slices,
oiled-side up, and cook for 5–6 minutes, or until
browned on one side. Turn the slices over and
cook on the other side until browned, then transfer
to a plate. Cut into bite-sized pieces.

Heat the remaining oil in a large saucepan over
a medium heat. Add the onion and peppers and
cook, stirring frequently, for 3–4 minutes until the
onion is just softened. Add the garlic and cook,
stirring frequently, for a further 2–3 minutes until
the onion is beginning to colour.

Add the tomatoes, chilli powder, cumin and
oregano and season to taste with salt and pepper.
Bring just to the boil, then reduce the heat, cover
and simmer gently for 15 minutes.

Add the courgettes, aubergine pieces, beans,
water and tomato purée to the saucepan and
return to the boil. Reduce the heat, cover
and simmer for a further 45 minutes, or until
the vegetables are tender. Taste and adjust the
seasoning, if necessary.

Ladle into warmed bowls and top with the spring
onions and cheese.

COOK'S TIP

*If you would prefer to leave
the purple aubergine skin
out of this chilli, you can
peel the aubergine before
cutting it into slices.*

serves 6 | prep 20 mins | cook 1 hr 40 mins–2 hrs

mexican three-bean chilli hotpot

INGREDIENTS

140 g/5 oz each dried black beans, cannellini
beans and pinto beans, soaked overnight in
separate bowls in water to cover
2 tbsp olive oil
1 large onion, finely chopped
2 red peppers, deseeded and diced
2 garlic cloves, very finely chopped
½ tsp cumin seeds, crushed
1 tsp coriander seeds, crushed
1 tsp dried oregano
½–2 tsp chilli powder
3 tbsp tomato purée
800 g/1 lb 12 oz canned chopped tomatoes
1 tsp sugar
1 tsp salt
600 ml/1 pint vegetable stock
3 tbsp chopped fresh coriander

Drain the beans, put in separate saucepans and cover with cold water. Bring to the boil and boil vigorously for 10–15 minutes, then reduce the heat and simmer for 35–45 minutes until just tender. Drain and set aside.

Heat the oil in a large, heavy-based saucepan over a medium heat. Add the onion and peppers and cook, stirring frequently, for 5 minutes, or until softened.

Add the garlic, cumin and coriander seeds and oregano and cook, stirring, for 30 seconds until the garlic is beginning to colour. Add the chilli powder and tomato purée and cook, stirring, for 1 minute. Add the tomatoes, sugar, salt, beans and stock.

Bring to the boil, then reduce the heat, cover and simmer, stirring occasionally, for 45 minutes.

Stir in the fresh coriander. Ladle into individual warmed bowls and serve at once.

serves 4 | prep 20 mins | cook 50 mins—1 hr

vegetable moussaka

INGREDIENTS
about 125 ml/4 fl oz olive oil
1 onion, chopped
4 celery sticks, chopped
1 garlic clove, finely chopped
400 g/14 oz canned chopped tomatoes
300 g/10½ oz canned green lentils
2 tbsp chopped fresh parsley
1 large aubergine, sliced
salt and pepper

TOPPING
25 g/1 oz butter
25 g/1 oz plain flour
300 ml/10 fl oz milk
pinch of freshly grated nutmeg
1 egg
55 g/2 oz freshly grated Parmesan cheese

Preheat the oven to 180°C/350°F/Gas Mark 4. Heat 1 tablespoon of the oil in a frying pan over a medium heat. Add the onion and cook, stirring frequently, for 5 minutes, or until softened. Add the celery, garlic, tomatoes, lentils and their can juices and parsley. Season to taste with salt and pepper. Reduce the heat, cover and simmer gently, stirring occasionally, for 15 minutes, or until the mixture has thickened.

Meanwhile, heat a little of the remaining oil in a large, heavy-based frying pan. Add the aubergine slices, in batches if necessary, and cook until golden on both sides, adding more oil as necessary. Remove with a slotted spoon and drain on kitchen paper. Layer an ovenproof dish with the lentil and tomato mixture and the aubergine slices, ending with a layer of aubergine.

To make the topping, put the butter, flour and milk in a saucepan over a medium—low heat and bring to the boil, whisking constantly. Season to taste with salt and pepper and nutmeg. Remove from the heat, leave to cool slightly, then beat in the egg. Pour the sauce over the aubergines, sprinkle with the Parmesan cheese and bake in the preheated oven for 30—40 minutes until golden on top. Serve at once.

VARIATION
For the traditional meat-eaters' version of this dish, substitute 350 g/12 oz fresh lamb mince for the lentils. Brown with the onions for 10 minutes.

serves 4 | prep 10 mins, plus 30 mins' soaking | cook 40 mins

vegetable lasagne

INGREDIENTS

40 g/1½ oz dried porcini mushrooms
2 tbsp olive oil
1 onion, finely chopped
400 g/14 oz canned chopped tomatoes
55 g/2 oz butter, plus extra for greasing
450 g/1 lb button mushrooms, thinly sliced
1 garlic clove, finely chopped
1 tbsp lemon juice
½ tsp Dijon mustard
¾ quantity cheese sauce
6 sheets no-precook lasagne
55 g/2 oz freshly grated Parmesan cheese
salt and pepper

Preheat the oven to 200°C/400°F/Gas Mark 6. Lightly grease an ovenproof dish. Put the porcini mushrooms in a small, heatproof bowl, cover with boiling water and leave to soak for 30 minutes. Meanwhile, heat the oil in a small frying pan over a medium heat. Add the onion and cook, stirring frequently, for 5 minutes, or until softened. Add the tomatoes and cook, stirring occasionally, for 7–8 minutes. Season to taste with salt and pepper and set aside.

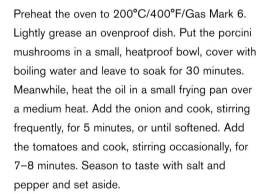

Drain and slice the porcini mushrooms. Melt half the butter in a large, heavy-based frying pan over a medium heat. Add the porcini and button mushrooms and cook, stirring, until they begin to release their juices. Reduce the heat to low, add the garlic and lemon juice and season to taste with salt and pepper. Cook, stirring occasionally, until almost all the liquid has evaporated.

Stir the mustard into the cheese sauce, then spread a layer over the base of the dish. Arrange a layer of lasagne sheets on top, cover with the mushrooms, another layer of sauce, another layer of lasagne, the tomato mixture and, finally, another layer of sauce. Sprinkle with the Parmesan cheese and dot with the remaining butter.

Bake in the preheated oven for 20 minutes. Leave to stand for 5 minutes before serving.

COOK'S TIP

Instead of grating the Parmesan cheese, you can shave off very thin strips using a vegetable peeler, to give a different consistency to the topping.

5

Salads are not just for summery days – with the wide variety of different flavoured and textured leaves freely available, you can enjoy them all year round. Salad leaves are particularly good with cheese, and here we have peppery rocket paired with smoked mozzarella slices and crisp cos with coarsely grated Parmesan.

SALADS

But traditional salad ingredients are only part of the picture. A range of vegetables and nuts are also imaginatively combined – courgettes with pine kernels, beetroot with pecan nuts, as well as French beans with walnuts. And fruit, too, makes an exciting culinary contribution in the vibrant Orange & Fennel Salad and the refreshing Pineapple & Cucumber Salad.

serves 4 | prep 15 mins | no cooking required

greek salad

INGREDIENTS
4 tomatoes, cut into wedges
1 onion, sliced
½ cucumber, sliced
225 g/8 oz kalamata olives, stoned
225 g/8 oz feta cheese, cubed
2 tbsp fresh coriander leaves
fresh flat-leaf parsley sprigs, to garnish
pitta bread, to serve

DRESSING
5 tbsp extra virgin olive oil
2 tbsp white wine vinegar
1 tbsp lemon juice
½ tsp sugar
1 tbsp chopped fresh coriander
salt and pepper

To make the dressing, put all the ingredients for the dressing into a large bowl and mix well together.

Add the tomatoes, onion, cucumber, olives, cheese and coriander. Toss all the ingredients together, then divide between individual serving bowls. Garnish with parsley sprigs and serve with pitta bread.

serves 4–6 | prep 10 mins, plus 3½ hrs' chilling | cook 10 mins

moorish courgette salad

INGREDIENTS
about 4 tbsp olive oil
1 large garlic clove, halved
500 g/1 lb 2 oz small courgettes, thinly sliced
55 g/2 oz pine kernels
55 g/2 oz raisins
3 tbsp finely chopped fresh mint leaves
  (not spearmint or peppermint)
about 2 tbsp lemon juice, or to taste
salt and pepper

Heat the oil in a large frying pan over a medium heat. Add the garlic and cook for 5 minutes, or until golden, to flavour the oil. Remove with a slotted spoon and discard. Add the courgettes and cook, stirring frequently, for 5 minutes, or until just tender. Immediately remove with a slotted spoon and transfer to a large serving bowl.

Add the pine kernels, raisins, mint, lemon juice and salt and pepper to taste to the courgettes and carefully stir to mix. Taste and add more oil, lemon juice and seasoning, if necessary.

Leave to cool completely, then cover with clingfilm and chill in the refrigerator for at least 3½ hours. Remove the salad from the refrigerator 10 minutes before serving.

COOK'S TIP
*This salad is best made
with young, tender courgettes
no more than 2.5 cm/1 inch
thick. If using older, larger
courgettes, cut them in half
or quarters lengthways first,
then thinly slice.*

serves 4 | prep 5 mins | cook 15 mins

warm potatoes with pesto

INGREDIENTS
450 g/1 lb small new potatoes
3 tsp pesto sauce
25 g/1 oz fresh grated Parmesan cheese
salt and pepper

Bring a large saucepan of salted water to the boil. Add the potatoes and cook for 15 minutes, or until tender. Drain, transfer to a salad bowl and leave to cool slightly.

Add the pesto sauce and salt and pepper to taste to the potatoes and toss together. Sprinkle with the Parmesan cheese and serve warm.

serves 4 | prep 15 mins | no cooking required

mozzarella salad with sun-dried tomatoes

INGREDIENTS

140 g/5 oz sun-dried tomatoes in olive oil
  (drained weight), oil from the jar reserved
15 g/½ oz fresh basil, roughly shredded
15 g/½ oz fresh flat-leaf parsley, roughly chopped
1 tbsp capers, rinsed
1 tbsp balsamic vinegar
1 garlic clove, roughly chopped
extra olive oil, if necessary
100 g/3½ oz mixed salad leaves, such as oakleaf
  lettuce, baby spinach and rocket
500 g/1 lb 2 oz smoked mozzarella, sliced
pepper

Put the sun-dried tomatoes, basil, parsley,
capers, vinegar and garlic in a food processor.
Measure the oil from the sun-dried tomatoes jar
and make it up to 150 ml/5 fl oz with more olive
oil, if necessary. Add it to the food processor
and process until smooth. Season to taste
with pepper.

Divide the salad leaves between 4 individual
serving plates. Top with the slices of mozzarella
and spoon over the dressing. Serve at once.

VARIATION

*Substitute Taleggio or
a soft goat's milk cheese
for the mozzarella.*

serves 4 | prep 15 mins | cook 10–15 mins

italian salad

INGREDIENTS

225 g/8 oz dried conchiglie
50 g/1¾ oz pine kernels
350 g/12 oz cherry tomatoes, halved
1 red pepper, deseeded and cut into
 bite-sized chunks
1 red onion, chopped
200 g/7 oz mozzarella di bufala, cut into
 small pieces
12 black olives, stoned
25 g/1 oz fresh basil leaves
fresh Parmesan cheese shavings, to garnish

DRESSING

5 tbsp extra virgin olive oil
2 tbsp balsamic vinegar
1 tbsp chopped fresh basil
salt and pepper

Bring a large saucepan of lightly salted water to the boil. Add the pasta, return to the boil and cook for 8–10 minutes until tender but still firm to the bite. Drain, refresh under cold running water and drain again. Leave to cool.

Meanwhile, heat a dry frying pan over a low heat, add the pine kernels and cook, shaking the pan frequently, for 1–2 minutes until lightly toasted. Remove from the heat, transfer to a dish and leave to cool.

To make the dressing, put all the ingredients for the dressing in a small bowl and mix well together. Cover with clingfilm and set aside.

To assemble the salad, divide the pasta between 4 serving bowls. Add the pine kernels, tomatoes, red pepper, onion, cheese and olives. Scatter over the basil, then drizzle over the dressing. Garnish with Parmesan cheese shavings and serve.

serves 4 | prep 10 mins | cook 15 mins

pasta salad with chargrilled peppers

INGREDIENTS
1 red pepper
1 orange pepper
280 g/10 oz dried conchiglie
5 tbsp extra virgin olive oil
2 tbsp lemon juice
2 tbsp pesto sauce
1 garlic clove
3 tbsp shredded fresh basil leaves
salt and pepper

Preheat the grill to medium–high. Arrange the peppers on a baking tray and cook under the grill, turning frequently, for 15 minutes, or until charred all over. Remove with tongs and transfer to a bowl. Cover with crumpled kitchen paper and set aside.

Meanwhile, bring a large saucepan of lightly salted water to the boil. Add the pasta, return to the boil and cook for 8–10 minutes until tender but still firm to the bite.

Combine the oil, lemon juice, pesto sauce and garlic in a large bowl, whisking well to mix. Drain the pasta, add it to the pesto mixture while still hot and toss well. Set aside.

When the peppers are cool enough to handle, peel off the skins. Halve, then remove and discard the seeds. Roughly chop the flesh and add to the pasta with the basil. Season to taste with salt and pepper and toss well. Serve at room temperature.

VARIATION
A more traditional salad, without the pasta, can be made in the same way. When the peppers have been under the grill for 10 minutes, add 4 tomatoes and grill for a further 5 minutes. Cover the peppers with kitchen paper, then peel and chop. Peel and roughly chop the tomatoes. Combine them with the dressing and garnish with black olives.

serves 4 | prep 5 mins | cook 5 mins

hot-&-sour noodle salad

INGREDIENTS
350 g/12 oz dried rice vermicelli noodles
4 tbsp sesame oil
3 tbsp soy sauce
juice of 2 limes
1 tsp sugar
4 spring onions, finely sliced
1–2 tsp hot chilli sauce
2 tbsp chopped fresh coriander

Prepare the noodles according to the packet instructions. Drain, put in a bowl and toss with half the oil.

Mix the remaining oil, soy sauce, lime juice, sugar, spring onions and chilli sauce together in a bowl. Stir into the noodles.

Stir in the coriander and serve.

serves 4 | prep 15 mins, plus 1 hr chilling | cook 5 mins

cauliflower & olive salad

INGREDIENTS
1 large cauliflower
225 g/8 oz stoned black olives, chopped
2 pimentos, chopped
2 tomatoes (optional)

DRESSING
175 ml/6 fl oz vegetable oil
3 tbsp white wine vinegar
1 garlic clove, crushed
salt and pepper

Break the cauliflower into florets. Bring a large saucepan of salted water to the boil. Add the cauliflower and cook for 5 minutes, or until just tender. Drain well.

Combine the cauliflower, olives and pimentos in a large bowl. If using tomatoes, quarter, deseed and chop the flesh. Add to the bowl with the other ingredients.

Put all the dressing ingredients in a screw-top jar and shake well. Pour the dressing over the salad and toss gently to coat. Cover with clingfilm and chill in the refrigerator for at least 1 hour.

Remove from the refrigerator 10 minutes before serving. Stir once more, then transfer to a dish and serve.

serves 4 | prep 15 mins, plus 20 mins' cooling | cook 20 mins

caesar salad

INGREDIENTS
1 garlic clove, halved
1 cos lettuce, separated into leaves
55 g/2 oz coarsely grated Parmesan cheese
2 eggs (optional)

GARLIC CROUTONS
3 tbsp olive oil
1 large garlic clove, halved
4 slices wholemeal bread, crusts removed,
  cut into cubes

DRESSING
1 egg (or 1 tbsp crème fraîche)
1 tsp vegetarian Worcestershire sauce
2 tbsp lemon juice
2 tsp Dijon mustard
2 tbsp olive oil
salt and pepper

Preheat the oven to 190°C/375°F/Gas Mark 5.
To make the croûtons, heat the oil with the garlic
in a small saucepan over a low heat for 5 minutes.
Remove and discard the garlic. Put the bread
cubes in a bowl, pour in the oil and toss to coat.
Spread the cubes out on a baking tray. Bake in
the preheated oven for 10 minutes, or until crisp.
Remove from the oven and leave to cool.

To make the dressing, put the egg in a saucepan
of water, bring to the boil and boil for 1 minute.
Remove with a slotted spoon. Crack the egg into
a bowl, scooping out any remaining egg white
from the shell. Whisk in the Worcestershire sauce,
lemon juice, mustard and oil and season to taste
with salt and pepper.

Rub the inside of a salad bowl with the garlic halves,
then discard. Arrange the lettuce leaves in the salad
bowl and sprinkle with the Parmesan cheese. Add
hard-boiled eggs, if desired. Drizzle the dressing
over the salad and sprinkle the garlic croûtons on
top. Toss the salad at the table and serve.

VARIATION
Add a pinch of cayenne
pepper and 1 teaspoon
paprika to the oil before
you bake the croûtons.

COOK'S TIP
For children, invalids and
pregnant women, substitute
crème fraîche for the lightly
cooked egg in the dressing
and add quartered hard-
boiled eggs to the salad.

serves 4 | prep 15 mins, plus 4 hrs' chilling | no cooking required

nutty beetroot salad

INGREDIENTS
3 cooked beetroot, grated
3 tbsp red wine vinegar or fruit vinegar
2 tart apples, such as Granny Smith
2 tbsp lemon juice

DRESSING
4 tbsp natural yogurt
4 tbsp mayonnaise
1 garlic clove, chopped
1 tbsp chopped fresh dill
salt and pepper

TO SERVE
4 large handfuls of mixed salad leaves
4 tbsp pecan nut halves

Put the beetroot in a non-metallic dish and sprinkle with the vinegar. Cover with clingfilm and chill in the refrigerator for at least 4 hours.

Core and slice the apples. Put in a dish. Sprinkle with the lemon juice to prevent discolouration.

To make the dressing, combine all the dressing ingredients in a small bowl. Remove the beetroot from the refrigerator and drizzle over the dressing. Add the apples to the beetroot and mix gently to coat with the dressing.

To serve, arrange a handful of salad leaves on each plate and top with a large spoonful of the apple and beetroot mixture.

Heat a dry frying pan over a medium heat, add the pecan nuts and cook, shaking the pan frequently, for 2 minutes, or until they begin to brown. Sprinkle the toasted nuts over the salad to garnish and serve at once.

serves 4 | prep 15 mins | no cooking required

good coleslaw

INGREDIENTS
½ **hard white cabbage**
2 **carrots**
2 **eating apples**
2 **celery sticks**
3 **spring onions**
150 ml/5 fl oz **mayonnaise**
150 ml/5 fl oz **natural yogurt**
1 tsp **French mustard**
2 tbsp **lemon juice**
40 g/1½ oz **raisins (optional)**
40 g/1½ oz **walnuts (optional)**

Finely shred the cabbage. Grate the carrots and core and slice the apples. Finely chop the celery and spring onions. Put in a large bowl.

Mix the mayonnaise and yogurt together in a small bowl. Whisk in the mustard and lemon juice and season well with salt and pepper.

Add the raisins and walnuts to the salad vegetables, if using. Pour over the dressing and mix well.

Serve at once.

serves 2 as a starter or 4 as a side dish | prep 10 mins, plus 30 mins' chilling | cook 5 mins

french bean & walnut salad

INGREDIENTS
450 g/1 lb French beans
1 small onion, finely chopped
1 garlic clove, chopped
4 tbsp freshly grated Parmesan cheese,
  plus extra to garnish
2 tbsp chopped walnuts or almonds, to garnish

DRESSING
6 tbsp olive oil
2 tbsp white wine vinegar
2 tsp chopped fresh tarragon
salt and pepper

Top and tail the beans, but leave them whole. Bring a saucepan of salted water to the boil. Add the beans and cook for 3–4 minutes. Drain well, refresh under cold running water and drain again. Put in a large bowl and add the onion, garlic and cheese.

Put all the dressing ingredients in a screw-top jar and shake well. Pour the dressing over the salad and toss gently to coat. Cover with clingfilm and chill in the refrigerator for at least 30 minutes.

Remove from the refrigerator 10 minutes before serving. Give the beans a brief stir and transfer to a shallow serving dish.

Heat a dry frying pan over a medium heat, add the nuts and cook, shaking the pan frequently, for 2 minutes, or until they begin to brown. Sprinkle the toasted nuts and Parmesan cheese over the beans to garnish and serve at once.

serves 6 | prep 15 mins | no cooking required

rocket & avocado salad

INGREDIENTS

1 red or green escarole lettuce, torn

½ frisée lettuce, torn

1 small bunch of watercress or mizuna

1 bunch of rocket, torn

1 red onion, thinly sliced into rings

2 oranges

1 avocado

55 g/2 oz walnuts, roughly chopped

DRESSING

6 tbsp olive oil

1 tbsp walnut oil

3 tbsp fresh lemon juice

2 tbsp fresh orange juice

1 tsp finely grated orange rind

1 tsp Dijon mustard

pinch of sugar

salt and pepper

COOK'S TIP

Always make sure that salad leaves are well dried after washing. Use a salad spinner, except for delicate leaves, or gently pat dry with kitchen paper or a tea towel.

To make the dressing, put all the ingredients for the dressing in a small bowl and whisk to mix.

Put the lettuces, watercress and rocket in a salad bowl. Separate the onion rings and add to the bowl. Working over the bowl to catch the juice, peel the oranges with a sharp knife and cut between the membranes to release the segments into the bowl.

Peel, stone and dice the avocado. Add to the salad. Pour over the dressing and toss well to coat. Sprinkle the walnuts over the top and serve.

VARIATION

For a milder nutty flavour, use 55 g/2 oz toasted pine kernels in place of the chopped walnuts, if you prefer.

serves 4 | prep 15 mins | no cooking required

avocado salad with lime dressing

INGREDIENTS

60 g/2¼ oz mixed red and green lettuce leaves

60 g/2¼ oz wild rocket

4 spring onions, finely diced

5 tomatoes, sliced

25 g/1 oz walnuts, toasted and chopped

2 avocados

1 tbsp lemon juice

LIME DRESSING

1 tbsp lime juice

1 tsp French mustard

1 tbsp crème fraîche

1 tbsp chopped fresh parsley or coriander

3 tbsp extra virgin olive oil

pinch of sugar

salt and pepper

Wash and drain the lettuce and rocket, if necessary. Shred all the leaves and arrange in the bottom of a large salad bowl. Add the spring onions, tomatoes and walnuts.

Peel, stone and thinly slice or dice the avocados. Brush them with the lemon juice to prevent discolouration, then transfer to the salad bowl. Gently mix together.

To make the dressing, put all the dressing ingredients in a screw-top jar and shake well. Drizzle over the salad and serve at once.

serves 4 | prep 15 mins | no cooking required

orange & fennel salad

INGREDIENTS

4 large, juicy oranges
1 large fennel bulb, very thinly sliced
1 mild white onion, finely sliced
2 tbsp extra virgin olive oil
12 plump black olives, stoned and thinly sliced
1 fresh red chilli, deseeded and very
 thinly sliced (optional)
finely chopped fresh parsley
French bread, to serve

Finely grate the rind of the oranges into a bowl and set aside. Working over a bowl to catch the juice, use a small serrated knife to remove all the white pith from the oranges. Cut the oranges horizontally into thin slices.

Toss the orange slices with the fennel and onion slices in a large bowl. Whisk the oil into the reserved orange juice, then spoon over the oranges. Scatter the olive slices over the top, add the chilli, if using, then sprinkle with the orange rind and parsley. Serve with French bread.

VARIATIONS

Garnet-red blood oranges
look stunning.

Juicy dark grapes make an
interesting alternative to
the olives.

serves 4 | prep 20 mins | no cooking required

pineapple & cucumber salad

INGREDIENTS

1 cucumber

1 small fresh pineapple

1 red onion, thinly sliced

1 bunch of watercress

DRESSING

3 tbsp lemon juice

2 tbsp soy sauce

1 tsp sugar

1 tsp chilli sauce

2 tbsp chopped fresh mint

Peel the cucumber and quarter lengthways. Scoop out the seeds with a teaspoon and discard. Cut each quarter into 1-cm/½-inch pieces. Put in a large bowl.

Peel the pineapple and quarter lengthways. Remove and discard the core. Cut each quarter in half lengthways, then cut into 1-cm/½-inch pieces. Add to the cucumber. Add the onion and watercress and toss together.

To make the dressing, put all the dressing ingredients in a small bowl and whisk together.

Pour the dressing over the salad and toss together. Transfer to a large serving platter and serve at once.

6

Nothing can be more appealing to the taste buds than the contrast between a crumbly, buttery pastry crust and a softly yielding vegetable filling, enriched with melting cheese or fluffy eggs, or both. Equally irresistible is a pizza fresh from the oven, with its crisp yet doughy base and piquant yet creamy topping.

TARTS, PIES & PIZZAS

Choose from a variety of pastry experiences, from the traditional rich shortcrust and airy puff to the crunchy filo. Or try the unusual walnut- and Parmesan cheese-enhanced tart cases. For something truly out-of-the-ordinary, plump for the Mushroom Gougère, with its choux pastry casing. More familiar but no less delicious is the scone-style topping of Winter Vegetable Cobbler.

serves 4 | prep 30 mins, plus 45 mins' chilling and cooling | cook 1 hr

spring vegetable tart

INGREDIENTS

PASTRY
250 g/9 oz plain flour, plus extra for dusting
pinch of salt
125 g/4½ oz cold butter, diced, plus extra for
  greasing
50 g/1¾ oz grated Parmesan cheese
1 egg
ice-cold water

FILLING
300 g/10½ oz selection of baby spring vegetables,
  such as carrots, asparagus, peas, broad beans,
  salad onions, sweetcorn and leeks
300 ml/10 fl oz double cream
125 g/4½ oz mature Cheddar cheese, grated
2 eggs plus 3 egg yolks
handful of tarragon and flat-leaf parsley, chopped
salt and pepper

Grease a 25-cm/10-inch loose-based tart tin. Sift the flour with the salt into a food processor, add the butter and process until the mixture resembles breadcrumbs. Tip into a large bowl and add the Parmesan cheese. Mix the egg and water together in a small bowl. Add most of the egg mixture and combine with a round-bladed knife or your fingertips to form a soft dough, adding more if necessary. Turn out onto a lightly floured work surface, roll out to 8 cm/3¼ inches larger than the tin and use to line the tin. Roll the rolling pin over the tin to neaten and trim the edge. Line the tart case with baking paper and fill with baking beans. Chill in the refrigerator for 30 minutes. Meanwhile, preheat the oven to 200°C/400°F/Gas Mark 6.

Bake the tart case in the preheated oven for 15 minutes. Remove the paper and beans and bake for a further 5 minutes. Remove from the oven and leave to cool. Reduce the oven temperature to 180°C/350°F/Gas Mark 4.

Prepare the vegetables where necessary, then cut into bite-sized pieces. Bring a large saucepan of lightly salted water to the boil. Add the vegetables and blanch for 2 minutes. Drain and leave to cool. Put the cream in a separate saucepan and bring to simmering point. Put the cheese, eggs and egg yolks in a heatproof bowl and pour over the hot cream. Add the herbs and salt and pepper to taste and stir to combine. Arrange the vegetables in the tart case, pour over the cheese custard and bake for 30–40 minutes until just set. Leave to cool in the tin for 10 minutes before serving.

COOK'S TIP
Use only the most tender
of young vegetables for this
tart. If they are really small,
you can leave them whole.
A few slices of soft goat's
cheese could be added just
before baking.

serves 4 | prep 40 mins, plus 1 hr chilling and cooling | cook 1¼ hrs

mushroom & onion quiche

INGREDIENTS
butter, for greasing
1 quantity rich shortcrust pastry dough, chilled
plain flour, for dusting

FILLING
55 g/2 oz unsalted butter
3 red onions, halved and sliced
350 g/12 oz mixed wild mushrooms, such as ceps,
  chanterelles and morels
2 tsp chopped fresh thyme
1 egg
2 egg yolks
100 ml/3½ fl oz double cream
salt and pepper

Preheat the oven to 190°C/375°F/Gas Mark 5. Lightly grease a 23-cm/9-inch loose-based quiche tin. Roll out the dough on a lightly floured work surface and use to line the tin. Line the pastry case with baking paper and fill with baking beans. Chill in the refrigerator for 30 minutes. Bake in the preheated oven for 25 minutes. Remove the paper and beans and cool on a wire rack. Reduce the oven temperature to 180°C/350°F/Gas Mark 4.

To make the filling, melt the butter in a large, heavy-based frying pan over a very low heat. Add the onions, cover and cook, stirring occasionally, for 20 minutes. Add the mushrooms and thyme and cook, stirring occasionally, for a further 10 minutes. Spoon into the pastry case and put the tin on a baking tray.

Lightly beat the egg, egg yolks, cream and salt and pepper to taste in a bowl. Pour over the mushroom mixture. Bake in the oven for 20 minutes, or until the filling is set and golden. Serve hot or at room temperature.

COOK'S TIP
If you are in a hurry, you can use ready-prepared shortcrust pastry dough, but, if it is frozen, make sure that you thaw it thoroughly before use.

VARIATION
Try making this quiche with other mushrooms, such as shiitake, field mushrooms or oyster mushrooms.

serves 4 | prep 15 mins | cook 25 mins

potato, fontina & rosemary tart

INGREDIENTS
1 quantity puff pastry
plain flour, for dusting

FILLING
3–4 waxy potatoes
300 g/10½ oz fontina cheese, cut into cubes
1 red onion, thinly sliced
3 large fresh rosemary sprigs
2 tbsp olive oil
1 egg yolk
salt and pepper

Preheat the oven to 190°C/375°F/Gas Mark 5.
Roll out the dough on a lightly floured work
surface into a round about 25 cm/10 inches
in diameter and put on a baking tray.

Peel the potatoes and slice as thinly as
possible so that they are almost transparent –
use a mandolin if you have one. Arrange the
potato slices in a spiral, overlapping the slices
to cover the pastry, leaving a 2-cm/¾-inch
margin around the edge.

Arrange the cheese and onion over the
potatoes, scatter with the rosemary and drizzle
over the oil. Season to taste with salt and
pepper and brush the edges with the egg yolk
to glaze.

Bake in the preheated oven for 25 minutes, or
until the potatoes are tender and the pastry is
brown and crisp.

serves 4 | prep 30 mins | cook 1 hr

lattice flan

INGREDIENTS
butter, for greasing
2 quantities rich shortcrust pastry dough,
** chilled**
plain flour, for dusting
lightly beaten egg, to glaze

FILLING
450 g/1 lb frozen spinach, thawed
2 tbsp olive oil
1 large onion, chopped
2 garlic cloves, finely chopped
2 eggs, lightly beaten
225 g/8 oz ricotta cheese
55 g/2 oz freshly grated Parmesan cheese
pinch of freshly grated nutmeg
salt and pepper

Preheat the oven to 200°C/400°F/Gas Mark 6. To make the filling, drain the spinach and squeeze out as much moisture as possible. Heat the oil in a large, heavy-based frying pan over a medium heat. Add the onion and cook, stirring frequently, for 5 minutes, or until softened. Add the garlic and spinach and cook, stirring occasionally, for 10 minutes. Remove from the heat and leave to cool slightly, then beat in the eggs and the ricotta and Parmesan cheeses. Season to taste with salt and pepper and nutmeg.

Lightly grease a 23-cm/9-inch loose-based flan tin. Roll out two-thirds of the dough on a lightly floured work surface and use to line the tin, leaving it overhanging the sides. Spoon in the spinach mixture, spreading it evenly over the base.

Roll out the remaining dough on a lightly floured work surface and cut into 5-mm/¼-inch strips. Arrange the strips in a lattice pattern on top of the flan, pressing the ends securely to seal. Trim any excess pastry. Brush with the egg to glaze and bake in the preheated oven for 45 minutes, or until golden brown. Transfer to a wire rack to cool slightly before removing from the tin.

COOK'S TIP
When preparing pastry for a flan tin, roll out away from you lightly in one direction only. Rotate the pastry in between strokes to ensure an even thickness.

makes 12 tartlets | prep 30 mins, plus 30 mins' chilling | cook 40 mins

stilton & walnut tartlets

INGREDIENTS
WALNUT PASTRY
225 g/8 oz plain flour, plus extra for dusting
pinch of celery salt
100 g/3½ oz cold butter, diced, plus extra
for greasing
25 g/1 oz walnut halves, chopped
ice-cold water

FILLING
25 g/1 oz butter
2 celery sticks, finely chopped
1 small leek, finely chopped
200 ml/7 fl oz double cream plus 2 tbsp
200 g/7 oz Stilton cheese
3 egg yolks
salt and pepper
fresh parsley, to garnish

Lightly grease a 7.5-cm/3-inch, 12-hole muffin tin. Sift the flour with the celery salt into a food processor, add the butter and process until the mixture resembles breadcrumbs. Tip into a large bowl and add the walnuts and a little cold water, just enough to bring the dough together. Turn out onto a lightly floured work surface and cut the dough in half. Roll out the first piece and cut out 6 x 9-cm/3½-inch rounds. Roll out each round to 12 cm/4½ inches in diameter and use to line the muffin holes. Repeat with the remaining dough. Line each hole with baking paper and fill with baking beans. Chill in the refrigerator for 30 minutes. Meanwhile, preheat the oven to 200°C/400°F/Gas Mark 6.

Bake the tartlet cases for 10 minutes. Remove from the oven, then remove the paper and beans.

To make the filling, melt the butter in a frying pan over a medium–low heat, add the celery and leek and cook, stirring occasionally, for 15 minutes until very soft. Add the 2 tablespoons of cream, crumble in the cheese and mix well. Season to taste with salt and pepper. Put the remaining cream in a saucepan and bring to simmering point. Pour onto the egg yolks in a heatproof bowl, stirring constantly. Mix in the cheese mixture and spoon into the tartlet cases. Bake for 10 minutes, then turn the tin around in the oven and bake for a further 5 minutes. Leave the tartlets to cool in the tin for 5 minutes. Serve garnished with parsley.

serves 4–6 | prep 10 mins, plus 10 mins' resting | cook 45–50 mins

caramelized onion tart

INGREDIENTS
100 g/3½ oz unsalted butter
600 g/1 lb 5 oz onions, thinly sliced
2 eggs
100 ml/3½ fl oz double cream
100 g/3½ oz grated Gruyère cheese
20-cm/8-inch ready-baked pastry case
100 g/3½ oz coarsely grated Parmesan cheese
salt and pepper

Melt the butter in a heavy-based frying pan over a medium heat. Add the onions and cook, stirring frequently to avoid burning, for 30 minutes, or until well-browned and caramelized. Remove the onions from the pan and set aside.

Preheat the oven to 190°C/375°F/Gas Mark 5. Beat the eggs in a large bowl, stir in the cream and season to taste with salt and pepper. Add the Gruyère and mix well. Stir in the cooked onions.

Pour the egg and onion mixture into the baked pastry case and sprinkle with the Parmesan cheese. Put on a baking tray. Bake in the preheated oven for 15–20 minutes until the filling has set and begun to brown.

Remove from the oven and leave to rest for at least 10 minutes. The tart can be served hot or left to cool to room temperature.

serves 4 | prep 20 mins, plus 10 mins' cooling | cook 1 hr

mushroom gougère

INGREDIENTS

CHOUX PASTRY

70 g/2½ oz strong white flour
pinch of salt
55 g/2 oz butter, plus extra for greasing
150 ml/5 fl oz water
2 eggs
55 g/2 oz Emmenthal cheese, grated

FILLING

2 tbsp olive oil
1 onion, chopped
225 g/8 oz chestnut mushrooms, sliced
2 garlic cloves, finely chopped
1 tbsp plain flour
150 ml/5 fl oz vegetable stock
85 g/3 oz walnuts, chopped
2 tbsp chopped fresh parsley
salt and pepper

Preheat the oven to 200°C/400°F/Gas Mark 6. To make the pastry, sift the flour with the salt onto a sheet of greaseproof paper. Melt the butter with the water in a saucepan over a medium heat, but do not let the mixture boil. Add the flour all at once and beat vigorously with a wooden spoon until the mixture is smooth and comes away from the side of the saucepan. Remove from the heat, leave to cool for 10 minutes, then gradually beat in the eggs until smooth and glossy. Beat in the cheese. Grease a round ovenproof dish and spoon the pastry around the side.

To make the filling, heat the oil in a large, heavy-based frying pan over a medium heat. Add the onion and cook, stirring frequently, for 5 minutes, or until softened. Add the mushrooms and garlic and cook, stirring, for 2 minutes. Stir in the flour and cook, stirring constantly, for 1 minute. Gradually stir in the stock. Bring to the boil, stirring constantly, and cook for 3 minutes, or until thickened. Reserve 2 tablespoons of the walnuts. Stir the remainder into the mushroom mixture with the parsley. Season to taste with salt and pepper.

Spoon the filling into the centre of the dish and sprinkle over the remaining walnuts. Bake in the preheated oven for 40 minutes, or until the pastry is risen and golden. Serve at once.

serves 4 | prep 30 mins | cook 40 mins

winter vegetable cobbler

INGREDIENTS

1 tbsp olive oil

1 garlic clove, crushed

8 small onions, halved

2 celery sticks, sliced

225 g/8 oz swede, chopped

2 carrots, sliced

½ small cauliflower, broken into florets

225 g/8 oz mushrooms, sliced

400 g/14 oz canned chopped tomatoes

55 g/2 oz red split lentils, rinsed and drained

2 tbsp cornflour

3–4 tbsp water

300 ml/10 fl oz vegetable stock

2 tsp Tabasco sauce

**2 tsp chopped fresh oregano, plus extra sprigs
to garnish**

TOPPING

225 g/8 oz self-raising flour

pinch of salt

4 tbsp butter

115 g/4 oz mature Cheddar cheese, grated

2 tsp chopped fresh oregano

1 egg, lightly beaten

150 ml/5 fl oz milk

VARIATION

*Substitute broccoli florets
for the cauliflower, or
chopped turnips for the
swede, if you prefer.*

Preheat the oven to 180°C/350°F/Gas Mark 4.
Heat the oil in a large frying pan over a low heat.
Add the garlic and onions and cook, stirring
frequently, for 5 minutes. Add the celery, swede,
carrots and cauliflower and cook, stirring, for
2–3 minutes. Add the mushrooms, tomatoes
and lentils.

Put the cornflour and water in a bowl and blend to
form a smooth paste. Stir into the frying pan with
the stock, Tabasco sauce and chopped oregano.
Transfer to an ovenproof dish, cover with foil and
bake in the preheated oven for 20 minutes.

Meanwhile, to make the topping, sift the flour
with the salt into a bowl. Add the butter and rub
into the flour with your fingertips until the mixture
resembles breadcrumbs. Stir in most of the
cheese and the chopped oregano. Beat the egg
with the milk in a small bowl and add enough to
the dry ingredients to make a soft dough. Turn out
onto a lightly floured work surface, knead briefly,
then roll out to a thickness of 1 cm/½ inch. Cut
into 5-cm/2-inch rounds.

Remove the dish from the oven and increase the
oven temperature to 200°C/400°F/Gas Mark 6.
Arrange the dough rounds around the edge of
the dish, brush with the remaining egg and milk
mixture and sprinkle with the remaining cheese.
Bake for a further 10–12 minutes. Garnish with
oregano sprigs and serve.

serves 6–8 | prep 20 mins, plus 40 mins' chilling, cooling and resting | cook 40 mins

leek & spinach pie

INGREDIENTS
1 quantity puff pastry
plain flour, for dusting
2 tbsp unsalted butter
2 leeks, finely sliced
225 g/8 oz fresh spinach leaves, chopped
2 eggs
300 ml/10 fl oz double cream
pinch of dried thyme
salt and pepper

Roll out the pastry on a lightly floured work surface
into a rectangle about 25 x 30 cm/10 x 12 inches.
Leave to rest for 5 minutes, then press the pastry
into a 20 x 25-cm/8 x 10-inch square flan dish,
leaving it overhanging the sides. Cover and chill
in the refrigerator while you make the filling.

Preheat the oven to 180°C/350°F/Gas Mark 4.
Melt the butter in a large frying pan over a medium
heat. Add the leeks and cook, stirring frequently,
for 5 minutes, or until softened. Add the spinach
and cook for 3 minutes, stirring frequently, until
wilted. Leave to cool.

Beat the eggs in a bowl. Stir in the cream, thyme
and salt and pepper to taste. Spread the cooked
vegetables over the base of the pastry case. Pour
in the egg mixture. Put on a baking sheet and
bake in the preheated oven for 30 minutes, or until
set. Remove from the oven and leave to rest for
10 minutes before serving. Serve directly from the
flan dish.

serves 6 | prep 25 mins, plus 45 mins' cooling and chilling | cook 1½ hrs

lentil, shallot & mushroom pie

INGREDIENTS

175 g/6 oz Puy or green lentils
2 bay leaves
6 shallots, sliced
1.2 litres/2 pints vegetable stock
55 g/2 oz butter
225 g/8 oz long-grain rice
8 sheets filo pastry, thawed if frozen
2 tbsp chopped fresh parsley
2 tsp chopped fresh fennel or savory
4 eggs, 1 beaten and 3 hard-boiled and sliced
225 g/8 oz field mushrooms, sliced
salt and pepper

Preheat the oven to 190°C/375°F/Gas Mark 5. Put the lentils, bay leaves and half the shallots in a large, heavy-based saucepan. Add half the stock and bring to the boil. Reduce the heat and simmer for 25 minutes, or until the lentils are tender. Remove from the heat, season to taste with salt and pepper and leave to cool completely.

Melt half the butter in a heavy-based saucepan over a medium heat, add the remaining shallots and cook, stirring frequently, for 5 minutes, or until softened. Stir in the rice and cook, stirring constantly, for 1 minute, then add the remaining stock. Season to taste with salt and pepper and bring to the boil. Reduce the heat, cover and simmer for 15 minutes. Remove from the heat and leave to cool completely.

Melt the remaining butter over a low heat, then brush an ovenproof dish with a little of it. Arrange the filo sheets in the dish, with the sides overhanging the dish (these will make the pie lid), brushing each sheet with melted butter. Add the parsley and fennel to the rice mixture, then beat in the beaten egg. Make layers of rice, hard-boiled egg, lentils and mushrooms in the dish, seasoning each layer to taste with salt and pepper. Bring up the filo sheets and scrunch into folds on top of the pie. Brush with melted butter and chill in the refrigerator for 15 minutes. Bake for 45 minutes. Leave to stand for 10 minutes before serving.

serves 4 | prep 20 mins | cook 1 hr 10 mins

potato-topped vegetables

INGREDIENTS

1 carrot, diced
175 g/6 oz cauliflower florets
175 g/6 oz broccoli florets
1 fennel bulb, sliced
85 g/3 oz French beans, halved
25 g/1 oz butter
25 g/1 oz plain flour
150 ml/5 fl oz vegetable stock
150 ml/5 fl oz dry white wine
150 ml/5 fl oz milk
175 g/6 oz chestnut mushrooms, quartered
2 tbsp chopped fresh sage

TOPPING

900 g/2 lb floury potatoes, diced
25 g/1 oz butter
4 tbsp natural yogurt
70 g/2½ oz freshly grated Parmesan cheese
1 tsp fennel seeds
salt and pepper

Preheat the oven to 190°C/375°F/Gas Mark 5. Bring a large saucepan of water to the boil, add the carrot, cauliflower, broccoli, fennel and beans and cook for 10 minutes, or until just tender. Drain and set aside.

Melt the butter in a saucepan over a low heat, add the flour and cook, stirring constantly, for 1 minute. Remove from the heat and stir in the stock, wine and milk. Return to the heat, bring to the boil and cook, stirring constantly, until thickened. Stir in the reserved vegetables, mushrooms and sage.

To make the topping, bring a large saucepan of water to the boil, add the potatoes and cook for 10–15 minutes until tender. Drain, return to the saucepan and add the butter, yogurt and half the cheese. Mash with a potato masher or a fork. Stir in the fennel seeds and salt and pepper to taste.

Spoon the vegetable mixture into a 1-litre/1¾-pint pie dish. Top with the potato mixture. Sprinkle over the remaining cheese. Bake in the preheated oven for 30–35 minutes until golden. Serve at once.

COOK'S TIP

For an extra creamy topping, mash the potatoes with the butter and yogurt and, before adding the cheese, beat for 1–2 minutes with a hand-held whisk.

serves 4 | prep 20 mins, plus 40 mins' chilling | cook 50 mins

cheese & vegetable pasties

INGREDIENTS

WHOLEMEAL PASTRY

225 g/8 oz plain wholemeal flour
pinch of salt
100 g/3½ oz butter, diced, plus extra for greasing
4 tbsp ice-cold water
2 tbsp milk, for glazing

FILLING

25 g/1 oz butter
1 onion, chopped
125 g/4½ oz potatoes, chopped
100 g/3½ oz carrots, chopped
25 g/1 oz French beans, chopped
100 ml/3½ fl oz water
2 tbsp canned and drained sweetcorn kernels
1 tbsp chopped fresh parsley
60 g/2¼ oz Cheddar cheese, grated
salt and pepper
salad leaves, to serve

To make the pastry, sift the flour with the salt into a large bowl. Add the butter and rub into the flour until the mixture resembles breadcrumbs. Add the water and combine with a round-bladed knife or your fingertips to form a soft dough. Shape the dough into a ball, wrap in foil and chill in the refrigerator for 40 minutes.

To make the filling, melt the butter in a large saucepan over a low heat. Add the onion, potatoes and carrots and cook, stirring frequently, for 5 minutes. Add the beans and water. Bring to the boil, then reduce the heat and simmer for 15 minutes. Remove from the heat and drain.

Refresh under cold running water, then drain again. Leave to cool.

Preheat the oven to 200°C/400°F/Gas Mark 6. Grease a baking tray. Cut the pastry into quarters and roll out on a lightly floured work surface into 4 rounds about 15 cm/6 inches in diameter. Mix the vegetables with the sweetcorn, parsley, cheese and salt and pepper to taste. Spoon onto one half of each pastry round. Brush the edges with water, then fold over and press together. Transfer to the prepared baking tray. Brush all over with milk to glaze. Bake in the preheated oven for 30 minutes until golden. Serve hot with salad leaves.

serves 2 | prep 10 mins | cook 15–20 mins

cheese & tomato pizza

INGREDIENTS

1 x 25-cm/10-inch pizza dough base

TOPPING

6 tomatoes, thinly sliced
175 g/6 oz mozzarella cheese, thinly sliced
2 tbsp shredded fresh basil leaves
2 tbsp olive oil, plus extra for brushing
salt and pepper

Preheat the oven to 230°C/450°F/Gas Mark 8. Brush a baking tray with oil and put the pizza dough base on it.

To make the topping, arrange the tomato and mozzarella cheese slices alternately over the dough. Season to taste with salt and pepper, sprinkle with the basil and drizzle with the oil.

Bake in the preheated oven for 15–20 minutes, until the crust is crisp and the cheese has melted. Serve at once.

serves 2 | prep 25 mins | cook 35–40 mins

pizza alla siciliana

INGREDIENTS
2 x 25-cm/10-inch pizza dough bases

TOMATO SAUCE
200 g/7 oz canned chopped tomatoes

5 tbsp passata

1 garlic clove, finely chopped

1 bay leaf

½ tsp dried oregano

½ tsp sugar

1 tsp balsamic vinegar

salt and pepper

TOPPING
1 aubergine, thinly sliced

2 tbsp olive oil, plus extra for brushing

175 g/6 oz mozzarella cheese, sliced

55 g/2 oz marinated, stoned black olives

1 tbsp capers, rinsed

4 tbsp freshly grated Parmesan cheese

Preheat the oven to 200°C/400°F/Gas Mark 6. Brush 2 baking trays with oil. To make the tomato sauce, put all the sauce ingredients in a heavy-based saucepan and bring to the boil. Reduce the heat and simmer, stirring occasionally, for 20 minutes, or until thickened and reduced. Remove from the heat, remove and discard the bay leaf and leave to cool.

Brush the aubergine slices with the oil, then spread out on 1 prepared baking tray. Bake in the preheated oven for 5 minutes, then turn the slices over and bake for a further 5–10 minutes. Transfer to kitchen paper to drain. Increase the oven temperature to 220°C/425°F/Gas Mark 7.

Brush the baking tray again with oil.

Put a pizza base on each of the prepared baking trays and divide the tomato sauce between them, spreading it almost to the edges. Arrange the aubergine on top and cover with the mozzarella cheese. Top with olives and capers and sprinkle with Parmesan cheese. Bake for 15–20 minutes, or until golden. Serve at once.

COOK'S TIP

For a really delicious topping, look for mozzarella di bufala – cheese made with water buffalo's milk – which has the finest flavour and texture.

VARIATION

If you like a nutty taste to your pizzas, substitute 25 g/1 oz pine kernels for the capers.

7

There is more to side dishes than potatoes alone, but they never fail to please, especially when cooked to crisp, golden perfection. Here you will learn how to achieve magnificent roast potatoes every time. You can then ring the changes with another spud special, the grated potato cake, Rösti.

SIDE DISHES

Discover some new ways with old favourites, such as Brussels Sprouts with Chestnuts – ideal for serving with a nut roast; Crispy Roast Asparagus with olive oil and Parmesan; French Beans with golden-toasted Pine Kernels; and Stir-fried Broccoli with ginger and chilli. Rice is also given a lift, with golden saffron and sweet spice or zesty lemon grass and creamy coconut milk.

serves 6 | prep 10 mins | cook 15 mins

sautéed garlic mushrooms

INGREDIENTS

450 g/1 lb button mushrooms
5 tbsp Spanish olive oil
2 garlic cloves, finely chopped
squeeze of lemon juice
4 tbsp chopped fresh flat-leaf parsley,
  plus extra sprigs to garnish
salt and pepper
crusty bread, to serve

Wipe or brush the mushrooms clean, then trim off the stalks close to the caps. Cut any large mushrooms in half or into quarters. Heat the oil in a large, heavy-based frying pan over a medium heat, add the garlic and cook, stirring, for 30 seconds–1 minute until lightly browned. Increase the heat to high, add the mushrooms and cook, stirring frequently, until the mushrooms have absorbed all the oil in the pan.

Reduce the heat to low. When the mushrooms have released their juices, increase the heat again and cook for 4–5 minutes, stirring frequently, until the juices have almost evaporated. Add the lemon juice and season to taste with salt and pepper. Stir in the parsley and cook for a further minute.

Transfer to a warmed serving dish and serve piping hot or warm, garnished with parsley sprigs. Accompany with chunks or slices of crusty bread for mopping up the garlic cooking juices.

VARIATIONS

Wild mushrooms, such as boletuses or chanterelles, can be used in place of cultivated mushrooms. Courgettes may also be prepared in the same way, with a finely chopped small onion cooked in the oil until lightly browned before adding the garlic.

serves 4 | prep 10 mins | cook 5 mins

garlic spinach stir-fry

INGREDIENTS
6 tbsp vegetable oil
6 garlic cloves, crushed
2 tbsp black bean sauce
3 tomatoes, roughly chopped
900 g/2 lb spinach, tough stalks removed,
 roughly chopped
1 tsp chilli sauce, or to taste
2 tbsp fresh lemon juice
salt and pepper

Heat the oil in a preheated wok or large frying pan over a high heat, add the garlic, black bean sauce and tomatoes and stir-fry for 1 minute.

Stir in the spinach, chilli sauce and lemon juice and mix well. Cook, stirring frequently, for 3 minutes, or until the spinach is just wilted. Season to taste with salt and pepper.

Remove from the heat and serve at once.

serves 8 | prep 10 mins | cook 20 mins

french beans with pine kernels

INGREDIENTS
2 tbsp Spanish olive oil
50 g/1¾ oz pine kernels
½–1 tsp paprika
450 g/1 lb French beans
1 small onion, finely chopped
1 garlic clove, finely chopped
juice of ½ lemon
salt and pepper

Heat the oil in a large, heavy-based frying pan over a medium–high heat, add the pine kernels and cook, stirring constantly and shaking the pan frequently, for 1 minute until light golden brown. Remove with a slotted spoon, drain well on kitchen paper, then transfer to a bowl. Reserve the oil in the frying pan. Add the paprika, to taste, to the pine kernels, stir together until coated and set aside.

Top and tail the beans. Put the beans in a saucepan and pour over boiling water to cover. Return to the boil and cook for 5 minutes, or until tender but still firm. Drain well in a colander.

Reheat the oil in the frying pan over a medium heat, add the onion and cook, stirring frequently, for 8–10 minutes until softened and beginning to brown. Add the garlic and cook, stirring, for a further 30 seconds.

Add the beans to the pan and cook, tossing together with the onion, for 2–3 minutes until heated through. Season the beans to taste with salt and pepper.

Turn the contents of the pan into a warmed serving dish, sprinkle over the lemon juice and toss together. Scatter over the pine kernels and serve hot.

serves 8 | prep 10 mins | cook 5½ hrs

boston beans

INGREDIENTS
500 g/1 lb 2 oz dried haricot beans, soaked
   overnight in water to cover
2 onions, chopped
2 large tomatoes, peeled and chopped
2 tsp American mustard
2 tbsp black treacle
salt and pepper

Preheat the oven to 140°C/275°F/Gas Mark 1.
Drain the beans and put in a large saucepan. Add
enough cold water to cover and bring to the boil.
Reduce the heat and simmer for 15 minutes.
Drain, reserving 300 ml/10 fl oz of the cooking
liquid. Transfer the beans to a large casserole and
add the onions.

Return the reserved cooking liquid to the
saucepan and add the tomatoes. Bring to the boil,
then reduce the heat and simmer for 10 minutes.
Remove from the heat, stir in the mustard and
treacle and season to taste with salt and pepper.

Pour the mixture into the casserole and bake in
the preheated oven for 5 hours. Serve at once.

VARIATION
If you are a meat-eater and
want to cook the original
one-pot meal, add 350 g/
12 oz diced salt pork to the
casserole with the onions.

serves 4 | prep 10 mins | cook 5 mins

mustard broccoli polonaise

INGREDIENTS
450 g/1 lb broccoli, cut into florets
55 g/2 oz butter
55 g/2 oz fresh breadcrumbs
1 tsp dry mustard powder
salt and pepper
1 hard-boiled egg, to garnish

Bring a large saucepan of salted water to the boil. Add the broccoli and cook for 5 minutes, or just until tender. Drain, refresh under cold running water and drain again. Transfer to a large serving dish. Season to taste with salt and pepper.

Meanwhile, melt the butter in a frying pan over a high heat, add the breadcrumbs and toss until well coated. Cook, stirring, for 1 minute, or until the crumbs are beginning to brown and crisp, then stir in the mustard powder.

Remove the breadcrumbs from the heat and sprinkle over the broccoli.

Shell and finely grate the hard-boiled egg. Scatter over the breadcrumbs to garnish. Serve hot.

serves 4 | prep 10 mins | cook 6–8 mins

stir-fried broccoli

INGREDIENTS

2 tbsp vegetable oil
2 broccoli heads, cut into florets
2 tbsp soy sauce
1 tsp cornflour
1 tbsp caster sugar
1 tsp grated fresh root ginger
1 garlic clove, crushed
pinch of dried chilli flakes
1 tsp toasted sesame seeds, to garnish

Heat the oil in a large preheated wok or frying pan over a high heat until almost smoking. Add the broccoli and stir-fry for 4–5 minutes. Reduce the heat to medium.

Combine the soy sauce, cornflour, sugar, ginger, garlic and chilli flakes in a small bowl. Add the mixture to the broccoli and cook, stirring constantly, for 2–3 minutes until the sauce thickens slightly.

Transfer to a warmed serving dish, garnish with the sesame seeds and serve at once.

serves 4 | prep 10 mins | cook 15–20 mins

brussels sprouts with chestnuts

INGREDIENTS
450 g/1 lb Brussels sprouts
115 g/4 oz unsalted butter
55 g/2 oz brown sugar
115 g/4 oz cooked and shelled chestnuts

Bring a large saucepan of salted water to the boil over a high heat.

Meanwhile, trim the Brussels sprouts and remove and discard any loose outer leaves. Add to the saucepan of water and boil for 5–10 minutes until just tender but not too soft. Drain well, refresh under cold water and drain again. Set aside.

Melt the butter in a heavy-based frying pan over a medium heat. Add the sugar and stir until dissolved.

Add the chestnuts and cook, stirring occasionally, until well coated and beginning to brown.

Add the sprouts to the chestnuts and mix well. Reduce the heat and cook gently, stirring occasionally, for 3–4 minutes to heat through.

Remove from the heat, transfer to a warmed serving dish and serve at once.

serves 4 | prep 10 mins | cook 20 mins

italian courgettes

INGREDIENTS
2 tbsp olive oil
1 large onion, chopped
1 garlic clove, finely chopped
5 courgettes, sliced
150 ml/5 fl oz vegetable stock
1 tsp chopped fresh marjoram
salt and pepper
1 tbsp chopped fresh flat-leaf parsley,
to garnish

Heat the oil in a large, heavy-based frying pan over a medium heat. Add the onion and garlic and cook, stirring frequently, for 5 minutes, or until softened. Add the courgettes and cook, stirring frequently, for 3–4 minutes, or until they are just beginning to brown.

Add the stock and marjoram and season to taste with salt and pepper. Simmer for 10 minutes, or until almost all the liquid has evaporated. Transfer to a warmed serving dish, sprinkle with the parsley and serve at once.

COOK'S TIP
Always leave the skin on courgettes, because this is where most of their nutrients are stored. They provide plenty of vitamin C as well as folic acid.

VARIATION
You can substitute other fresh herbs of your choice for the marjoram and parsley to bring a slightly different flavour to this dish.

serves 4 | prep 5 mins | cook 10–15 mins

crispy roast asparagus

INGREDIENTS
450 g/1 lb asparagus spears
2 tbsp extra virgin olive oil
1 tsp coarse sea salt
1 tbsp freshly grated Parmesan cheese, to serve

Preheat the oven to 200°C/400°F/Gas Mark 6. Choose asparagus spears of similar widths. Trim the base of the spears so that all the stems are approximately the same length.

Arrange the asparagus in a single layer on a metal baking tray. Drizzle with oil and sprinkle with salt.

Bake in the preheated oven for 10–15 minutes, turning once. Transfer to a warmed serving dish and serve at once, sprinkled with the grated Parmesan cheese.

roasted root vegetables

INGREDIENTS

3 parsnips, peeled and cut into 5-cm/2-inch
 pieces
4 baby turnips, quartered
3 carrots, peeled and cut into 5-cm/2-inch pieces
450 g/1 lb butternut squash, peeled and cut into
 5-cm/2-inch chunks
450 g/1 lb sweet potato, peeled and cut into
 5-cm/2-inch chunks
2 garlic cloves, finely chopped
2 tbsp chopped fresh rosemary
2 tbsp chopped fresh thyme
2 tsp chopped fresh sage
3 tbsp olive oil
salt and pepper
2 tbsp chopped mixed fresh herbs, such as
 parsley, thyme and mint, to garnish

Preheat the oven to 220°C/425°F/Gas Mark 7.
Arrange all the prepared vegetables in a single
layer in a large roasting tin. Scatter over the garlic
and herbs.

Pour over the oil and season well with salt and
pepper. Toss all the ingredients together until they
are well mixed and coated with the oil (you can
leave them to marinate at this stage to allow the
flavours to be absorbed).

Roast at the top of the preheated oven for
50 minutes–1 hour until the vegetables are
cooked and browned, turning over halfway
through the cooking time. Serve hot, scattered
with mixed fresh herbs to garnish.

VARIATIONS

*Shallots or wedges of red
onion can be added to the
root vegetables to give
additional flavour and
texture. Whole cloves of
unpeeled garlic are also
good roasted with the other
vegetables. You can then
squeeze out the creamy
cooked garlic flesh over
the roasted vegetables
when eating them.*

serves 6 | prep 10 mins | cook 50–55 mins

perfect roast potatoes

INGREDIENTS

1.3 kg/3 lb large, floury potatoes, such as King Edward, Maris Piper or Desirée, peeled and cut into even-sized chunks
3 tbsp olive oil
salt

VARIATION

Small, whole, unpeeled new potatoes are delicious roasted, too. They don't need any parboiling – just coat them with the hot oil and then roast for 30–40 minutes. Drain well and season to taste with salt and pepper before serving.

Preheat the oven to 220°C/425°F/Gas Mark 7. Bring a large saucepan of salted water to the boil, add the potatoes and cook, covered, for 5–7 minutes. They will still be firm. Remove from the heat.

Meanwhile, add the oil to a roasting tin and heat in the preheated oven.

Drain the potatoes well and return to the saucepan. Cover with the lid and firmly shake the saucepan so that the surface of the potatoes is roughened, to help give a much crisper texture.

Remove the roasting tin from the oven and carefully tip the potatoes into the hot oil. Baste to ensure that they are all well coated with the oil.

Roast at the top of the preheated oven for 45–50 minutes until the potatoes are browned all over and thoroughly crisp, turning only once halfway through the cooking time and basting, otherwise the crunchy edges will be destroyed.

Carefully transfer the potatoes to a warmed serving dish. Sprinkle with a little salt and serve at once. Any leftovers are delicious cold.

serves 4 | prep 15 mins | cook 1–1½ hours

caramelized sweet potatoes

INGREDIENTS
450 g/1 lb sweet potatoes
55 g/2 oz butter, plus extra for greasing
55 g/2 oz brown sugar, maple syrup or honey
2 tbsp orange or pineapple juice
55 g/2 oz pineapple pieces (optional)
pinch of ground cinnamon, nutmeg or
  mixed spice (optional)

Scrub the sweet potatoes, but do not peel. Bring a large saucepan of salted water to the boil. Add the sweet potatoes and cook for 30–45 minutes, depending on their size, until just tender. Remove from the heat and drain well. Leave to cool slightly, then peel.

Preheat the oven to 200°C/400°F/Gas Mark 6. Thickly slice the sweet potatoes and arrange in a single overlapping layer in a greased ovenproof dish. Cut the butter into small cubes and dot over the top.

Sprinkle with the sugar and fruit juice. Add the pineapple and spices, if using.

Bake in the preheated oven, basting occasionally, for 30–40 minutes until golden brown. Serve hot.

serves 6 | prep 10 mins | cook 20 mins

feisty potatoes

INGREDIENTS
CHILLI OIL
150 ml/5 fl oz olive oil
2 small fresh red chillies, split
1 tsp hot Spanish paprika

POTATOES
2 tbsp olive oil
1 kg/2 lb 4 oz potatoes, unpeeled, cut into chunks
mayonnaise, to serve

To make the chilli oil, heat the oil and chillies in a
heavy-based frying pan over a high heat until the
chillies begin to sizzle. Remove from the heat and
stir in the paprika. Set aside and leave to cool,
then transfer the oil to a pourer with a spout.
Do not sieve.

Heat the olive oil in a large, heavy-based frying
pan over a medium heat, add the potatoes and
cook, stirring occasionally, for 15 minutes until
golden brown all over and tender. Remove with
a slotted spoon and transfer to a plate covered
in kitchen paper. Blot off the excess oil.

To serve, divide the potatoes between 6 serving
plates and add a dollop of mayonnaise to each.
Drizzle with the chilli oil and serve warm or at
room temperature. In Spain, these potatoes are
traditionally served with wooden cocktail sticks.

serves 4 | prep 15 mins, plus 1 hr cooling and chilling | cook 30 mins

rösti

INGREDIENTS
900 g/2 lb potatoes, unpeeled
25–55 g/1–2 oz unsalted butter or vegan
  margarine
1–2 tbsp olive oil
salt and pepper

Bring a large saucepan of water to the boil, add
the potatoes and cook for 10 minutes. Drain and
leave to cool completely. Cover and chill in the
refrigerator for at least 30 minutes.

Peel and coarsely grate the potatoes. Melt
25 g/1 oz of the butter with 1 tablespoon of the
oil in a heavy-based, 23-cm/9-inch frying pan over
a medium heat. Spread out the grated potato
evenly in the frying pan, reduce the heat and cook
for 10 minutes.

Cover the frying pan with a large plate and
carefully invert the frying pan and plate together
so that the potato cake drops onto the plate.
Add more butter and oil, if necessary, and carefully
slide the potato cake back into the frying pan to
cook the second side for a further 10 minutes.
Season to taste with salt and pepper and serve
at once.

COOK'S TIP
Chilling the parboiled
potatoes in the refrigerator
is not essential, but it will
make them easier to handle
when you grate them.

serves 4 | prep 10 mins | cook 25–30 mins

asian coconut rice

INGREDIENTS

2 tbsp vegetable oil
1 onion, chopped
400 g/14 oz long-grain rice, rinsed and drained
1 tbsp freshly chopped lemon grass
500 ml/18 fl oz coconut milk
400 ml/14 fl oz water
6 tbsp flaked coconut, toasted

Heat the oil in a large saucepan over a low heat, add the onion and cook, stirring frequently, for 3 minutes. Add the rice and lemon grass and cook, stirring, for a further 2 minutes.

Stir in the coconut milk and water and bring to the boil. Reduce the heat, cover and simmer for 20–25 minutes until all the liquid has been absorbed. If the rice grains have not cooked through, add a little more water and cook until tender and all the liquid has been absorbed.

Remove from the heat and add half the flaked coconut. Stir gently. Scatter over the remaining coconut flakes and serve.

golden rice

INGREDIENTS

1 tsp saffron threads

2 tbsp hot water

2 tbsp ghee or vegetable oil

3 onions, chopped

3 tbsp butter

1 tsp ground cumin

1 tsp ground cinnamon

1 tsp salt

½ tsp pepper

½ tsp paprika

3 bay leaves

400 g/14 oz long-grain rice, rinsed and drained

about 850 ml/1½ pints vegetable stock or water

100 g/3½ oz cashew nut halves, toasted

Put the saffron threads and hot water into a small bowl and set aside to soak.

Meanwhile, heat the ghee in a large saucepan over a low heat, add the onions and cook, stirring frequently, for 5 minutes. Add the butter, cumin, cinnamon, salt, pepper, paprika and bay leaves and cook, stirring, for 2 minutes. Add the rice and cook, stirring, for 3 minutes. Add the saffron and its soaking liquid and pour in the stock. Bring to the boil, then reduce the heat, cover and simmer for 20–25 minutes until all the liquid has been absorbed. If the rice grains have not cooked through, add a little more stock and cook until tender and all the liquid has been absorbed.

Remove from the heat and remove and discard the bay leaves. Taste and adjust the seasoning, if necessary. Add the cashew nuts and stir well. Serve hot.

8

Desserts have an often well-deserved reputation for being wicked indulgences, overladen with fat, sugar and calories. But the following recipes offer a good balance between providing a sweet treat and avoiding excess, majoring as they do on luscious fresh fruit, with the odd concession to the chocoholics.

DESSERTS

Grilled Fruit Kebabs present a fast-food feast of eye-catching exotic fruits, while spiced pears and apricots are simply left to bake in their glorious juices. More sumptuous is the all-time favourite Lemon Meringue Pie and a citrusy twist on the traditional rice pudding. Chilled temptations include the immortal Tiramisù and the aromatic Coconut & Ginger Ice Cream.

makes about 1 litre or 1¾ pints | prep 10 mins, plus 45 mins–8½ hrs' freezing and softening | no cooking required

easy mango ice cream

INGREDIENTS
600 ml/1 pint ready-made traditional custard
150 ml/5 fl oz whipping cream, lightly whipped
flesh of 2 ripe mangoes, puréed
icing sugar, to taste (optional)
passion fruit pulp, to serve

Mix the custard, cream and mango purée together in a large bowl.

Taste for sweetness and, if necessary, add icing sugar to taste, remembering that when frozen, the mixture will taste less sweet.

Transfer to an ice cream maker and process for 15 minutes. Alternatively, transfer the mixture to a freezerproof container. Cover and freeze for 2–3 hours until just frozen. Spoon into a bowl and beat with a fork or whisk to break down any ice crystals. Return the mixture to the container and freeze for a further 2 hours. Beat the ice cream once more, then freeze for 2–3 hours until firm.

Transfer from the freezer to the refrigerator 20–30 minutes before serving to soften. Serve with the passion fruit pulp.

serves 4 | prep 10 mins, plus 1¼–9 hrs' chilling and freezing | cook 5 mins

chocolate gelato

INGREDIENTS
6 egg yolks
100 g/3½ oz caster sugar
350 ml/12 fl oz milk
175 ml/6 fl oz double cream
90 g/3¼ oz cooking chocolate, grated
pieces of flaked chocolate or Caraque, to decorate

Beat the egg yolks and sugar in a large, heatproof bowl until fluffy. Pour the milk, cream and grated chocolate into a large saucepan and bring to the boil. Remove from the heat and whisk into the egg yolk mixture. Pour back into the saucepan and cook, stirring, over a very low heat until thickened. Do not let it simmer. Transfer to a bowl and leave to cool. Cover with clingfilm and chill in the refrigerator for 1 hour.

Transfer to an ice cream maker and process for 15 minutes. Alternatively, transfer the mixture to a freezerproof container. Cover and freeze for 2–3 hours until just frozen. Spoon into a bowl and beat with a fork or whisk to break down any ice crystals. Return the mixture to the container and freeze for a further 2 hours. Beat the ice cream once more, then freeze for 2–3 hours until firm.

To make Caraque, melt some chocolate in a heatproof bowl set over a saucepan of simmering water, then spread it over an acrylic board and leave to set. Scrape a knife over the chocolate.

To serve, scoop the gelato into serving dishes. Decorate with flaked chocolate or Caraque.

makes about 1 litre or 1½ pints | prep 20 mins, plus 1¼–9 hrs' cooling, freezing and softening | cook 10 mins

coconut & ginger ice cream

INGREDIENTS

400 ml/14 fl oz coconut milk
250 ml/9 fl oz whipping cream
4 egg yolks
5 tbsp caster sugar
4 tbsp syrup from the stem ginger
6 pieces stem ginger, drained and finely chopped
2 tbsp lime juice
orange zest, to decorate

TO SERVE
lychees
ginger syrup

Heat the coconut milk and cream in a saucepan over a medium–low heat until just beginning to simmer. Remove from the heat.

Beat the egg yolks, sugar and ginger syrup together in a large bowl until pale and creamy. Slowly pour in the hot milk mixture, stirring constantly. Return to the saucepan and heat over a medium–low heat, stirring constantly, until the mixture thickens and coats the back of a spoon. Remove from the heat and leave to cool. Stir in the ginger and lime juice.

Transfer to an ice cream maker and process for 15 minutes. Alternatively, transfer the mixture to a freezerproof container. Cover and freeze for 2–3 hours until just frozen. Spoon into a bowl and beat with a fork or whisk to break down any ice crystals. Return the mixture to the container and freeze for a further 2 hours. Beat the ice cream once more, then freeze for 2–3 hours until firm.

Transfer from the freezer to the refrigerator 20–30 minutes before serving to soften. Decorate with grated orange zest. Serve with lychees and a little ginger syrup drizzled over.

serves 4–6 | prep 10 mins, plus 1–6¾ hrs cooling, freezing and softening | cook 5 mins

lemon sorbet with cava

INGREDIENTS
3–4 lemons
250 ml/9 fl oz water
200 g/7 oz caster sugar
fresh mint sprigs, to garnish
1 bottle Spanish cava, chilled, to serve

Roll the lemons on the work surface, pressing firmly, which helps to extract as much juice as possible. Pare off a few strips of rind and reserve for decoration, if desired, then finely grate the rind from 3 lemons. Squeeze the juice from as many of the lemons as necessary to give 175 ml/6 fl oz.

Put the water and sugar in a heavy-based saucepan over a medium–high heat and stir to dissolve the sugar. Bring to the boil, without stirring, and boil for 2 minutes. Remove from the heat and stir in the grated lemon rind. Cover and leave to stand for 30 minutes, or until cool.

When the mixture is cool, stir in the lemon juice. Strain into an ice cream maker and process according to the manufacturer's instructions. Alternatively, strain the mixture into a freezerproof container and freeze for 2 hours, or until mushy and freezing around the edges. Tip into a bowl and beat. Return to the freezer and repeat the process twice more. Remove the sorbet from the freezer 10 minutes before serving to soften.

Serve in scoops, decorated with the reserved lemon zest, if using, and mint sprigs, with a little of the cava poured over.

VARIATION
You can serve the lemon sorbet in frozen hollow lemon shells. To do this, slice the tops off 4–6 lemons and use a sharp teaspoon to scoop out the fruit. Spoon the almost-frozen sorbet into the lemons and put upright in the freezer until frozen.

serves 6 | prep 10 mins, plus 9 hrs' standing, cooling and chilling | cook 1¼–1½ hrs

spanish caramel custard

INGREDIENTS
500 ml/18 fl oz full-fat milk
½ orange, with 2 pared strips of the rind
1 vanilla pod, split, or ½ tsp vanilla essence
175 g/6 oz caster sugar
4 tbsp water
butter, for greasing
3 large eggs plus 2 large egg yolks

Pour the milk into a saucepan and add the orange rind and vanilla pod. Bring to the boil, then remove from the heat and stir in 100 g/3½ oz of the sugar. Leave to stand for at least 30 minutes to infuse.

Meanwhile, put the remaining sugar and the water in a separate saucepan over a medium–high heat. Stir until the sugar dissolves, then boil without stirring until the caramel turns deep golden brown.

Immediately remove the saucepan from the heat and squeeze in a few drops of juice from the orange to prevent further cooking. Pour into a lightly greased 1.2-litre/2-pint soufflé dish and swirl to cover the base. Set aside.

Preheat the oven to 160°C/325°F/Gas Mark 3. When the milk has infused, return the saucepan to the heat and bring the milk to a simmer. Beat the eggs and egg yolks together in a bowl. Pour the warm milk into the eggs, whisking constantly. Strain into the soufflé dish.

Put the soufflé dish in a roasting tin and pour in enough boiling water to come halfway up the side of the dish. Bake in the preheated oven for 1¼–1½ hours until set and a knife inserted in the centre comes out clean.

Remove the soufflé dish from the roasting tin and set aside to cool completely. Cover and chill in the refrigerator overnight.

To serve, run a metal spatula around the side of the dish, then invert onto a serving plate with a rim, shaking firmly to release.

serves 6 | prep 30 mins, plus 3½ hrs' chilling | cook 20 mins

fine chocolate tart

INGREDIENTS
CHOCOLATE PASTRY
125 g/4½ oz plain flour, plus extra for dusting
2 tsp cocoa powder, plus extra for dusting
2 tsp icing sugar
pinch of salt
50 g/1¾ oz cold butter, diced
1 egg yolk
ice-cold water
pieces of flaked white and plain chocolate or
  Caraque, to decorate

GANACHE FILLING
200 g/7 oz plain chocolate with 70% cocoa solids
25 g/1 oz unsalted butter, softened
225 ml/8 fl oz double cream
1 tsp dark rum (optional)

Lightly grease a 23-cm/9-inch loose-based fluted tart tin. Sift the flour, cocoa powder, icing sugar and salt into a food processor, add the butter and process until the mixture resembles breadcrumbs. Tip the mixture into a large bowl and add the egg yolk and a little ice-cold water, just enough to bring the dough together. Turn out onto a work surface dusted with extra flour and cocoa powder, roll out to 8 cm/3¼ inches larger than the tin and use to line the tin. Roll the rolling pin over the tin to neaten and trim the edge. Line the tart case with baking paper and fill with baking beans. Chill in the refrigerator for 30 minutes. Meanwhile, preheat the oven to 190°C/375°F/Gas Mark 5.

Bake the tart case in the preheated oven for 15 minutes. Remove the paper and beans and bake for a further 5 minutes.

To make the ganache filling, chop the chocolate and put in a heatproof bowl with the softened butter. Bring the cream to the boil in a saucepan, then pour over the chocolate, stirring constantly. Add the rum, if using, and continue stirring until the chocolate is completely melted. Pour into the tart case and chill in the refrigerator for 3 hours. Decorate with flaked chocolate or Caraque.

serves 4 | prep 15 mins | cook 10–15 mins

banana-stuffed crêpes

INGREDIENTS
225 g/8 oz plain flour
2 tbsp soft light brown sugar
2 eggs
450 ml/16 fl oz milk
grated rind and juice of 1 lemon
55 g/2 oz butter
3 bananas
4 tbsp golden syrup

Combine the flour and sugar in a large bowl. Make a well in the centre, add the eggs and half the milk to the well and gradually beat in, drawing in the flour mixture from the sides. Beat together until smooth. Gradually beat in the remaining milk to make a smooth batter. Stir in the lemon rind.

Melt a little of the butter in a 20-cm/8-inch frying pan over a high heat. Pour in one-quarter of the batter. Tilt the frying pan to coat the base and cook for 1–2 minutes until set. Flip the crêpe over and cook the second side. Slide out of the frying pan and keep warm in a low oven. Repeat to make 3 more crêpes.

Slice the bananas and put in a bowl. Toss in the lemon juice to prevent discolouration. Pour over the syrup and toss together. Fold each crêpe into 4 and fill the centre with the banana mixture. Serve warm.

serves 4 | prep 10 mins, plus 10 mins' marinating | cook 10 mins

grilled fruit kebabs

INGREDIENTS
2 tbsp hazelnut oil
2 tbsp clear honey
juice and finely grated rind of 1 lime
2 pineapple rings, halved
8 strawberries
1 pear, peeled, cored and thickly sliced
1 banana, peeled and thickly sliced
2 kiwi fruit, peeled and quartered
1 star fruit, cut into 4 slices

Preheat the grill to medium. Mix the oil, honey and lime juice and rind together in a large, shallow, non-metallic dish. Add the fruit and turn to coat. Cover and leave to marinate for 10 minutes.

Thread the fruit alternately onto 4 long metal skewers, beginning with a piece of pineapple and ending with a slice of star fruit.

Brush the kebabs with the marinade and cook under the grill, brushing frequently with the marinade, for 5 minutes. Turn the kebabs over, brush with the remaining marinade and grill for a further 5 minutes. Serve at once.

COOK'S TIP

Honey varies widely in flavour and the best quality, with a distinctive taste, is usually made from a single type of blossom. For this recipe, try orange blossom, acacia or lime flower.

VARIATION

You can use other types of fruit for these kebabs, such as seedless grapes, mango slices and pawpaw chunks.

serves 4 | prep 5 mins | cook 30 mins

spiced baked pears

INGREDIENTS
4 large, firm eating pears
150 ml/5 fl oz apple juice
1 cinnamon stick
4 whole cloves
1 bay leaf

Preheat the oven to 180°C/350°F/Gas Mark 4.

Peel and core the pears, then quarter. Put in an ovenproof dish and add the remaining ingredients.

Cover the dish and bake in the preheated oven for 30 minutes.

Serve the pears hot or cold.

serves 4 | prep 10 mins | cook 12–15 mins

baked apricots with honey

INGREDIENTS
butter, for greasing
4 apricots, halved and stoned
4 tbsp flaked almonds
4 tbsp honey
pinch of ground ginger or grated nutmeg
vanilla ice cream, to serve (optional)

Preheat the oven to 200°C/400°F/Gas Mark 6.
Lightly grease an ovenproof dish large enough to
hold the apricot halves in a single layer.

Arrange the apricot halves in the dish, cut-sides
up. Sprinkle with the almonds and drizzle over the
honey. Dust with the spice.

Bake in the preheated oven for 12–15 minutes
until the apricots are tender and the almonds
golden. Remove from the oven and serve at once,
with ice cream on the side, if desired.

serves 6 | prep 15 mins | cook 25–30 mins

rhubarb crumble

INGREDIENTS
900 g/2 lb rhubarb
115 g/4 oz caster sugar
grated rind and juice of 1 orange
cream, yogurt or custard, to serve

CRUMBLE
225 g/8 oz plain or wholemeal flour
115 g/4 oz butter
115 g/4 oz soft light brown sugar
1 tsp ground ginger

Preheat the oven to 190°C/375°F/Gas Mark 5.

Cut the rhubarb into 2.5-cm/1-inch lengths and put in a 1.7-litre/3-pint ovenproof dish with the sugar and orange rind and juice.

To make the crumble, put the flour in a bowl, add the butter and rub into the flour with your fingertips until the mixture resembles breadcrumbs. Stir in the sugar and ginger.

Spread the crumble evenly over the fruit and press down lightly with a fork.

Put on a baking tray. Bake in the centre of the preheated oven for 25–30 minutes until the crumble is golden brown.

Serve warm with cream, yogurt or custard.

serves 4–6 | prep 10 mins | cook 30 minutes

rice pudding

INGREDIENTS
1 large orange
1 lemon
1 litre/1¾ pints milk
250 g/9 oz Spanish short-grain rice
100 g/3¾ oz caster sugar
1 vanilla pod, split
pinch of salt
125 ml/4 fl oz double cream
soft light brown sugar, to serve (optional)

Finely grate the rinds from the orange and lemon and set aside. Rinse a heavy-based saucepan with cold water, but do not dry it.

Put the milk and rice in the saucepan over a medium–high heat and bring to the boil. Reduce the heat, stir in the caster sugar, vanilla pod, orange and lemon rinds and salt and simmer, stirring frequently, until the pudding is thick and creamy and the rice grains are tender. This can take up to 30 minutes, depending on how wide the saucepan is.

Remove the vanilla pod and stir in the cream. Serve at once, sprinkled with brown sugar, if desired, or leave to cool completely, cover and chill until required. (The pudding will thicken as it cools, so stir in extra milk, if necessary.)

serves 4 | prep 20 mins, plus 2 hrs' chilling | no cooking required

tiramisù

INGREDIENTS
200 ml/7 fl oz strong black coffee,
  cooled to room temperature
4 tbsp orange liqueur, such as Cointreau
3 tbsp orange juice
16 Italian sponge fingers
250 g/9 oz mascarpone cheese
300 ml/10 fl oz double cream, lightly whipped
3 tbsp icing sugar
grated rind of 1 orange
60 g/2¼ oz chocolate, grated

TO DECORATE
chopped toasted almonds
crystallized orange peel

Pour the cooled coffee into a jug and stir in the orange liqueur and orange juice. Put half the sponge fingers in the base of a serving dish, then pour over half the coffee mixture.

Put the mascarpone cheese in a separate bowl with the cream, icing sugar and orange rind and mix well together. Spread half the mascarpone mixture over the coffee-soaked sponge fingers, then arrange the remaining sponge fingers on top. Pour over the remaining coffee mixture and then spread over the remaining mascarpone mixture. Scatter over the grated chocolate.

Chill in the refrigerator for at least 2 hours. Serve decorated with chopped toasted almonds and crystallized orange peel.

serves 6 | prep 30 mins, plus 1½ hrs' chilling | cook 1½ hrs

toffee apple tart

INGREDIENTS
butter, for greasing
plain flour, for dusting
1 quantity rich shortcrust pastry dough, chilled
thick cream to serve

FILLING
1.3 kg/3 lb Cox's Orange Pippin or other firm,
  sweet apples, peeled and cored
1 tsp lemon juice
50 g/1¾ oz butter
100 g/3½ oz caster sugar
200 g/7 oz granulated sugar
90 ml/3 fl oz cold water
150 ml/5 fl oz double cream
icing sugar, for dusting (optional)

Lightly grease a 23-cm/9-inch loose-based fluted tart tin. Roll out the dough on a lightly floured work surface and use to line the tin. Roll the rolling pin over the tin to neaten and trim the edge. Line with baking paper and fill with baking beans. Chill in the refrigerator for 30 minutes. Meanwhile, preheat the oven to 190°C/375°F/Gas Mark 5.

Bake the tart case in the preheated oven for 10 minutes. Remove the paper and beans. Bake for a further 5 minutes.

Meanwhile, take 4 apples, cut each one into 8 pieces and toss in the lemon juice to prevent discolouration. Melt the butter in a frying pan over a medium heat, add the apple pieces and cook until just beginning to caramelize on the edges. Remove from the pan and leave to cool.

Thinly slice the remaining apples, put them in a saucepan with the caster sugar and cook for 20–30 minutes until soft. Spoon the cooked apple slices into the tart case and arrange the reserved apple pieces on top in a circle. Bake for 30 minutes.

Put the granulated sugar and water in a saucepan and heat until the sugar dissolves. Boil until caramelized. Remove from the heat and add the cream, stirring constantly to combine into toffee. Remove the tart from the oven, pour the toffee over the apples and chill in the refrigerator for 1 hour. When ready to serve, sift icing sugar over the tart, if desired. Serve with thick cream.

serves 8–10 | prep 30 mins, plus 45 mins' chilling | cook 50 mins

lemon meringue pie

INGREDIENTS
butter, for greasing
1 quantity rich shortcrust pastry dough, chilled
plain flour, for dusting
3 tbsp cornflour
85 g/3 oz caster sugar
grated rind of 3 lemons
300 ml/10 fl oz cold water
150 ml/5 fl oz lemon juice
3 egg yolks
55 g/2 oz unsalted butter, diced

MERINGUE
3 egg whites
175 g/6 oz caster sugar
1 tsp golden granulated sugar

Grease a 25-cm/10-inch fluted flan tin. Roll out the pastry on a lightly floured work surface to a round 5 cm/2 inches larger than the flan tin and use to line the tin. Roll the rolling pin over the tin to neaten and trim the edge. Prick the base of the flan case with a fork and chill, uncovered, in the refrigerator for 20–30 minutes.

Preheat the oven to 200°C/400°F/Gas Mark 6. Preheat a baking tray. Line the pastry case with baking paper and fill with baking beans. Put on the preheated baking tray and bake in the preheated oven for 15 minutes. Remove the paper and beans and bake for a further 10 minutes until the pastry is dry and just colouring. Remove from the oven and reduce the oven temperature to 150°C/300°F/Gas Mark 2.

Put the cornflour, sugar and lemon rind in a saucepan. Pour in a little of the water and blend to a smooth paste. Gradually add the remaining water and the lemon juice. Put the saucepan over a medium heat and bring the mixture to the boil, stirring constantly. Reduce the heat and simmer gently for 1 minute until smooth and glossy. Remove from the heat. Beat in the egg yolks, one at a time, then beat in the butter. Put the saucepan in a bowl of cold water to cool the filling. When cool, spoon the mixture into the pastry case.

To make the meringue, whisk the egg whites using an electric mixer until thick and soft peaks form. Gradually add the caster sugar, whisking well after each addition. The mixture should be glossy and firm. Spoon the meringue over the filling to cover it completely and make a seal with the pastry case. Swirl the meringue into peaks and sprinkle with the granulated sugar.

Bake for 20–30 minutes until the meringue is crisp and pale gold (the centre should still be soft). Leave to cool slightly before serving.

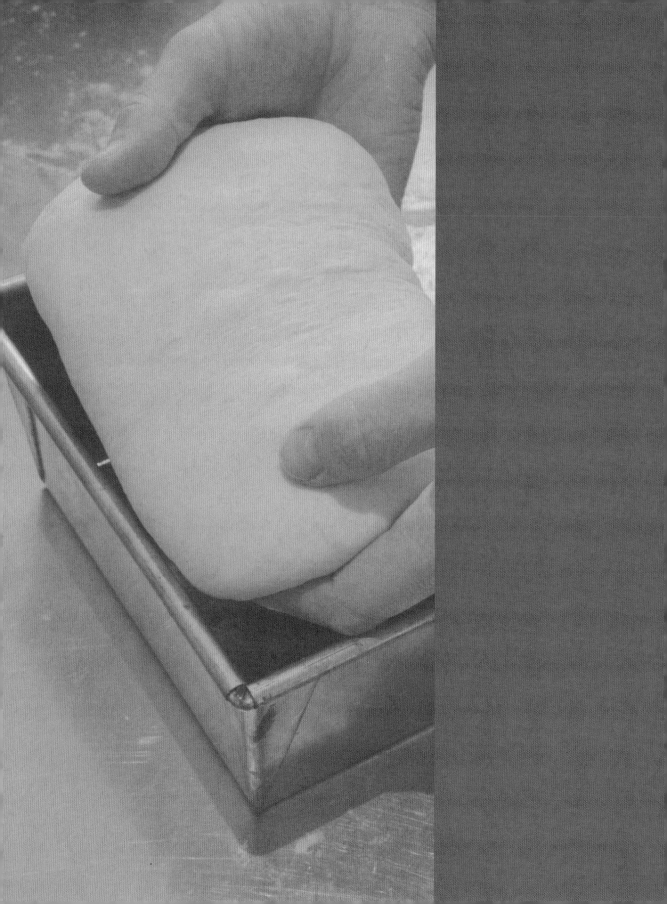

9

Freshly baked bread, with its heavenly aroma and taste, has to be one of the best, and simplest, eating pleasures, and these basic, no-nonsense recipes are sure to give you both the inspiration and the confidence to make your own delicious loaves. You really can achieve great results with minimal effort!

BREADS, CAKES & BISCUITS

You may, however, be more inclined to put your baking efforts into the sweet rather than the savoury, but the rewards will be equally satisfying. Featured are the great cake classics, such as the decorative Coffee & Walnut Cake and the dense Rich Chocolate Cake, while other teatime treats include dainty Almond Biscuits and chewy Hazelnut & Almond Oaties.

makes 1 large loaf or 8 baps | prep 20 mins, plus 1½ hrs' proving | cook 15–30 mins

fresh bread

INGREDIENTS
butter, for greasing
450 g/1 lb strong plain flour, plus extra
for dusting
1 tsp salt
1 x 7 g/⅛ oz sachet easy-blend dried yeast
1 tbsp vegetable oil or melted butter
350 ml/12 fl oz tepid water

Grease a 900-g/2-lb loaf tin or 2 baking trays.

Mix the flour, salt and yeast together in a large bowl. Make a well in the centre, add the oil and water to the well and gradually mix in, drawing in the flour mixture from the sides, to form a soft dough.

Use a free-standing electric mixer to knead the dough with the dough hook for 4–5 minutes. Alternatively, turn the dough out onto a lightly floured work surface and knead well for 5–7 minutes. The dough should have a smooth appearance and feel elastic.

Return the dough to the bowl, cover with clingfilm and leave in a warm place to rise for 1 hour, or until the dough has doubled in size.

Turn out onto the work surface and knead again until smooth. For a loaf shape, shape as a rectangle the length of the loaf tin and 3 times the width. Fold the dough into 3 and put into the prepared tin with the join underneath so that you have a well-shaped loaf. Alternatively, divide the dough into 8 equal pieces, shape into rounds and space well apart on the prepared baking trays. Dust with a little extra flour for a softer crust. Cover with clingfilm and leave to rise again in a warm place for 30 minutes, or until the loaf is well risen above the tin or the baps are doubled in size.

Meanwhile, preheat the oven to 230°C/450°F/ Gas Mark 8. If baking a loaf, bake in the centre of the preheated oven for 25–30 minutes until cooked through – it should sound hollow when tapped on the bottom. If the top is getting too brown, reduce the temperature a little. For the baps, bake for 15–20 minutes, swapping the baking trays around halfway through the cooking time. Transfer to wire racks to cool. Eat the bread as fresh as possible.

makes 2 small loaves | prep 20 mins, plus 2¼ hrs' proving | cook 40 mins

olive & sun-dried tomato bread

INGREDIENTS

400 g/14 oz plain flour, plus extra for dusting
1 tsp salt
1 x 7 g/⅛ oz sachet easy-blend dried yeast
1 tsp brown sugar
1 tbsp chopped fresh thyme
4 tbsp olive oil, plus extra for oiling
200 ml/7 fl oz warm water (heated to 50°C/122°F)
50 g/1¾ oz black olives, stoned and sliced
50 g/1¾ oz green olives, stoned and sliced
100 g/3½ oz sun-dried tomatoes in olive oil,
  drained and sliced
1 egg yolk, beaten

Mix the flour, salt and yeast together in a large bowl, then stir in the sugar and thyme. Make a well in the centre, add most of the oil and water to the well and gradually mix in, drawing in the flour mixture from the sides, to form a soft dough. Add the remaining oil and water, if necessary. Mix in the olives and sun-dried tomatoes. Turn the dough out onto a lightly floured work surface and knead well for 5 minutes, then shape into a ball. Brush the bowl with oil and return the dough to the bowl. Cover with clingfilm and leave in a warm place to rise for 1½ hours, or until the dough has doubled in size.

Dust a baking tray with flour. Turn the dough out on the work surface and knead lightly again. Cut in half and shape each half into an oval or round. Put on the prepared baking tray, cover with clingfilm and leave to rise again in a warm place for 45 minutes, or until doubled in size.

Meanwhile, preheat the oven to 200°C/400°F/Gas Mark 6. Make 3 shallow, diagonal cuts in the top of each piece of dough. Brush with the egg. Bake in the preheated oven for 40 minutes, or until cooked through – they should be golden on top and sound hollow when tapped on the bottom. Transfer to wire racks to cool. Store in an airtight container for up to 3 days.

irish soda bread

INGREDIENTS
butter, for greasing
450 g/1 lb plain flour, plus extra for dusting
1 tsp salt
1 tsp bicarbonate of soda
400 ml/14 fl oz buttermilk

Preheat the oven to 220°C/425°F/Gas Mark 7.
Grease a baking tray.

Sift the flour, salt and bicarbonate of soda into a
large bowl. Make a well in the centre, add most
of the buttermilk to the well and gradually mix in,
drawing in the flour mixture from the sides, to form
a very soft but not too wet dough. Add the
remaining buttermilk, if necessary.

Turn the dough out onto a lightly floured work
surface and knead lightly. Shape into a 20-cm/
8-inch round.

Put the dough on the prepared baking tray, cut a
cross in the top and bake in the preheated oven
for 25–30 minutes until cooked through – it
should sound hollow when tapped on the bottom.
Eat while still warm. Soda bread is always best
eaten the same day as it is made.

VARIATIONS

*Add 1 tablespoon chopped
fresh rosemary and 55 g/
2 oz sultanas. For a change,
make with Granary flour and
add a handful of seeds or
coarse oatmeal, or make
with half stoneground flour
and half white flour and
55 g/2 oz chopped walnuts.
Sweet soda bread can be
made with the addition of
25 g/1 oz sugar and 85 g/
3 oz mixed dried fruits. This
is known as 'spotted dog'.
Another sweet version can
be made with the addition
of 1 tablespoon sugar and
85 g/3 oz roughly chopped
plain chocolate.*

makes 8 | prep 25 mins, plus 1 hr 40 mins standing and proving | cook 10 mins

naan breads

INGREDIENTS
1 tsp fresh yeast
about 150 ml/5 fl oz warm water
1 tsp sugar
200 g/7 oz plain flour, plus extra for dusting
1 tsp salt
3 tbsp ghee or vegetable oil
1 tsp chilli powder
½ tsp ground coriander

Mix the yeast, water and sugar together in a bowl and leave to stand for 10 minutes.

Sift the flour with the salt into a separate bowl. Make a well in the centre, add 1 tablespoon of the ghee and the yeast mixture to the well and gradually mix in, drawing in the flour from the sides, to form a smooth dough. Shape into a ball. Turn out onto a lightly floured work surface. Knead for 5 minutes. Return to the bowl, cover and leave in a warm place to rise for 1½ hours, or until doubled in size.

Knead the dough again for 3 minutes. Divide into 8 pieces and shape each piece into a ball. Flatten into ovals 5 mm/¼ inch thick. Mix the chilli powder and coriander together, then turn the naan breads in the spice mixture until evenly coated.

Preheat the grill to high. Line a grill rack with foil and brush with ghee. Arrange the naans on top and brush with ghee. Cook under the grill for 10 minutes, turning and brushing with the remaining ghee. Serve hot.

scones

INGREDIENTS

450 g/1 lb plain flour, plus extra for dusting
½ tsp salt
2 tsp baking powder
55 g/2 oz butter
2 tbsp caster sugar
250 ml/9 fl oz milk, plus extra for glazing
strawberry jam and clotted cream, to serve

Preheat the oven to 220°C/425°F/Gas Mark 7.
Sift the flour, salt and baking powder into a bowl.
Add the butter and rub into the flour mixture with
your fingertips until the mixture resembles
breadcrumbs. Stir in the sugar.

Make a well in the centre, add the milk to the well
and gradually stir in with a round-bladed knife to
form a soft dough.

Turn out the dough onto a lightly floured work
surface and lightly flatten until it is of an even
thickness, about 1 cm/½ inch. Don't be heavy-
handed – scones need a light touch.

Use a 6-cm/2½-inch pastry cutter to cut out the
scones and put on a baking tray.

Brush with a little milk to glaze. Bake in the
preheated oven for 10–12 minutes until golden
and well risen.

Transfer to a wire rack to cool. Serve freshly baked
with the traditional accompaniments of strawberry
jam and clotted cream.

VARIATIONS

*To make fruit scones,
add 55 g/2 oz mixed fruit
with the sugar. To make
wholemeal scones, use
wholemeal flour and omit the
sugar. These are delicious
to serve with soup or as an
accompaniment to cheese.
To make cheese scones,
omit the sugar and fruit and
add 55 g/2 oz finely grated
Cheddar or Double
Gloucester cheese to the
mixture with 1 teaspoon
of dry mustard powder.*

makes 6 bars | prep 20 mins, plus 40 mins' cooling | cook 55 mins

carrot cake

INGREDIENTS

butter, for greasing
100 g/3½ oz self-raising flour
pinch of salt
1 tsp ground mixed spice
½ tsp ground nutmeg
125 g/4½ oz soft light brown sugar
2 eggs, beaten
5 tbsp sunflower oil
125 g/4½ oz carrots, peeled and grated
1 banana, chopped
25 g/1 oz chopped toasted mixed nuts

ICING

40 g/1½ oz butter, softened
3 tbsp cream cheese
175 g/6 oz icing sugar, sifted
1 tsp fresh orange juice
grated rind of ½ orange
walnut halves or pieces, to decorate

Preheat the oven to 190°C/375°F/Gas Mark 5. Grease an 18-cm/7-inch square cake tin and line with baking paper.

Sift the flour, salt, mixed spice and nutmeg into a bowl. Stir in the brown sugar, then stir in the eggs and oil. Add the carrots, banana and nuts and mix well together.

Spoon the mixture into the prepared tin and level the surface. Bake in the preheated oven for 55 minutes, or until golden and just firm to the touch. Leave to cool slightly. When cool enough to handle, turn out onto a wire rack and leave to cool completely.

To make the icing, put the butter, cream cheese, icing sugar and orange juice and rind in a bowl and beat together until creamy. Spread the icing over the top of the cold cake, then use a fork to make shallow, wavy lines in the icing. Scatter over the walnuts, cut the cake into bars and serve.

makes 10–12 slices | prep 25 mins, plus 40 mins' soaking and cooling | cook 45 mins

rich chocolate cake

INGREDIENTS

100 g/3½ oz raisins

finely grated rind and juice of 1 orange

175 g/6 oz butter, diced, plus extra for greasing

**100 g/3½ oz plain chocolate, at least 70% cocoa
solids, broken into pieces**

4 large eggs, beaten

100 g/3½ oz caster sugar

1 tsp vanilla essence

55 g/2 oz plain flour

55 g/2 oz ground almonds

½ tsp baking powder

pinch of salt

**55 g/2 oz blanched almonds, lightly toasted
and chopped**

icing sugar, sifted, to decorate

Preheat the oven to 180°C/350°F/Gas Mark 4. Line a deep, loose-based, 25-cm/10-inch round cake tin with greaseproof paper. Grease the paper.

Put the raisins in a small bowl, add the orange juice and leave to soak for 20 minutes.

Melt the butter and chocolate together in a small saucepan over a medium heat, stirring. Remove from the heat and set aside to cool.

Using an electric mixer, beat the eggs, sugar and vanilla essence together for 3 minutes, or until light and fluffy. Stir in the cooled chocolate mixture.

Drain the raisins if they have not absorbed all the orange juice. Sift the flour, ground almonds, baking powder and salt into the egg and sugar mixture. Add the raisins, orange rind and almonds and fold all the ingredients together.

Spoon into the cake tin and smooth the surface. Bake in the preheated oven for 40 minutes, or until a cocktail stick inserted into the centre comes out clean and the cake starts to come away from the side of the tin. Leave to cool in the tin for 10 minutes, then remove from the tin, transfer to a wire rack and leave to cool completely. Dust the surface with icing sugar before serving.

serves 4 | prep 20 mins, plus 2½ hrs' cooling and chilling | cook 1 hr

coffee & walnut cake

INGREDIENTS

ICING

6 tbsp organic cocoa powder

2 tbsp cornflour

6 tbsp caster sugar

125 ml/4 fl oz strong black coffee, cooled

250 ml/9 fl oz milk

SPONGE

275 g/9½ oz plain flour

1 tbsp baking powder

85 g/3 oz caster sugar

85 g/3 oz butter, softened, plus extra for greasing

2 eggs

150 ml/5 fl oz milk

3 tbsp hot strong black coffee

60 g/2¼ oz walnuts, chopped

50 g/1¾ oz sultanas

walnut halves, to decorate

To make the icing, put all the icing ingredients into a blender or food processor and process until creamy. Transfer to a saucepan and heat, stirring, over a medium heat until bubbling. Cook for 1 minute, then pour into a heatproof bowl. Leave to cool, then cover with clingfilm and chill in the refrigerator for at least 2 hours.

Preheat the oven to 190°C/375°F/Gas Mark 5. Grease a 23-cm/9-inch loose-based cake tin and line with baking paper. To make the sponge, sift the flour with the baking powder into a bowl, then stir in the sugar. In a separate bowl, beat the butter, eggs, milk and coffee together, then mix into the flour mixture. Stir in the chopped walnuts and the sultanas. Spoon into the prepared cake tin and level the surface. Bake in the preheated oven for 1 hour. Leave to cool slightly. When cool enough to handle, turn out onto a wire rack and leave to cool completely. Spread the icing over the top of the cold cake, decorate with the walnut halves and serve.

makes 12–18 pieces | prep 15 mins, plus 15 mins' cooling | cook 1 hr 35 mins

gingerbread

INGREDIENTS
450 g/1 lb plain flour
3 tsp baking powder
1 tsp bicarbonate of soda
3 tsp ground ginger
175 g/6 oz butter
175 g/6 oz soft light brown sugar
175 g/6 oz black treacle
175 g/6 oz golden syrup, plus extra
  to serve (optional)
1 egg, beaten
300 ml/10 fl oz milk
cream, to serve (optional)

Preheat the oven to 160°C/325°F/Gas Mark 3.
Line a 23-cm/9-inch square cake tin, 5 cm/
2 inches deep, with greaseproof paper or
baking paper.

Sift the dry ingredients into a large bowl.

Put the butter, sugar, treacle and syrup in a
medium saucepan over a low heat and heat until
the butter has melted and the sugar has dissolved.
Leave to cool a little. Mix the beaten egg with the
milk and add to the cooled syrup mixture.

Add all the liquid ingredients to the flour mixture
and beat well using a wooden spoon until the
mixture is smooth and glossy.

Pour the mixture into the prepared tin and bake in
the centre of the preheated oven for 1½ hours
until well risen, just firm to the touch and a skewer
inserted into the centre of the cake comes out

clean. This gives a lovely sticky gingerbread, but
if you prefer a firmer cake, bake for a further
15 minutes.

Remove from the oven and leave the cake to cool
in the tin. When cool, remove the cake from the tin
with the lining paper. Wrap in foil and store in an
airtight tin for up to 1 week to allow the flavours
to mature.

Cut into wedges and serve for tea or serve with
cream as a pudding. Extra warmed syrup is an
added extravagance.

makes 30 | prep 15 mins | cook 10 mins

orange cream cheese cookies

INGREDIENTS
225 g/8 oz butter or margarine,
** plus extra for greasing**
200 g/7 oz light muscovado sugar
85 g/3 oz cream cheese
1 egg, lightly beaten
350 g/12 oz plain flour
1 tsp bicarbonate of soda
1 tbsp fresh orange juice
1 tsp finely grated orange rind,
** plus extra for decorating**
demerara sugar, for sprinkling

Preheat the oven to 190°C/375°F/Gas Mark 5. Grease a large baking tray.

Put the butter, sugar and cream cheese in a large bowl and beat until light and fluffy. Beat in the egg. Sift in the flour and bicarbonate of soda and add the orange juice and rind. Mix well.

Drop about 30 rounded tablespoonfuls of the mixture onto the prepared baking tray, making sure that they are well spaced. Sprinkle with the demerara sugar.

Bake in the preheated oven for 10 minutes, or until the cookies are light brown at the edges.

Leave to cool on a wire rack. Decorate with orange rind before serving.

makes 36 | prep 10 mins | cook 12 mins

hazelnut & almond oaties

INGREDIENTS

175 g/6 oz butter or margarine, plus extra
 for greasing
140 g/5 oz demerara sugar
1 egg
100 g/3½ oz plain flour
½ tsp salt
1 tsp bicarbonate of soda
¼ tsp almond essence
125 g/4½ oz rolled oats
40 g/1 oz hazelnuts, roughly chopped
40 g/1 oz almonds, roughly chopped
175 g/6 oz plain chocolate chips

Preheat the oven to 190°C/375°F/Gas Mark 5. Grease a large baking tray.

Put the butter and sugar in a large bowl and beat until light and fluffy. Beat in the egg.

Sift the flour, salt and bicarbonate of soda into a separate bowl, then stir into the butter mixture.

Add the almond essence and oats and beat thoroughly. Stir in the nuts and chocolate chips.

Put 36 teaspoonfuls of the mixture onto the prepared baking tray, making sure that they are well spaced. Bake in the preheated oven for 12 minutes, or until the oaties are golden brown.

Leave to cool on a wire rack before serving.

makes about 60 | prep 15 minutes | cook 15–20 minutes

almond biscuits

INGREDIENTS
150 g/5½ oz butter, at room temperature,
  plus extra for greasing
150 g/5½ oz caster sugar
115 g/4 oz plain flour
25 g/1 oz ground almonds
pinch of salt
75 g/2¾ oz blanched almonds, lightly toasted and
  finely chopped
finely grated rind of 1 large lemon
4 egg whites

Preheat the oven to 180°C/350°F/Gas Mark 4.
Grease 1 or more baking trays. Put the butter and
sugar into a bowl and beat until light and fluffy. Sift
in the flour, ground almonds and salt, tipping in
any ground almonds left in the sieve. Use a large
metal spoon to fold in the chopped almonds and
lemon rind.

Whisk the egg whites in a separate clean, grease-
free bowl until soft peaks form. Fold the egg
whites into the almond mixture.

Drop small teaspoonfuls of the mixture onto the
prepared baking trays, making sure that they are
well spaced. (You may need to bake in batches.)
Bake in the preheated oven for 15–20 minutes
until golden brown at the edges. Leave to cool
on a wire rack before serving.

makes 24 | prep 10 mins, plus 30 mins' chilling | cook 12 mins

nutty chocolate drizzles

INGREDIENTS
225 g/8 oz butter or margarine,
  plus extra for greasing
275 g/9½ oz demerara sugar
1 egg
140 g/5 oz plain flour, sifted
1 tsp baking powder
1 tsp bicarbonate of soda
125 g/4½ oz rolled oats
20 g/¾ oz bran
20 g/¾ oz wheatgerm
115 g/4 oz mixed nuts, toasted
  and roughly chopped
90 g/3¼ oz plain chocolate chips
115 g/4 oz raisins and sultanas
175 g/6 oz plain chocolate, roughly chopped

Preheat the oven to 180°C/350°F/Gas Mark 4.
Grease a large baking tray. Put the butter, sugar
and egg in a large bowl and beat until light and
fluffy. Add the flour, baking powder, bicarbonate of
soda, oats, bran and wheatgerm and mix together
until well combined. Stir in the nuts, chocolate
chips and dried fruit.

Put 24 rounded tablespoonfuls of the mixture
onto the prepared baking tray. Bake in the
preheated oven for 12 minutes, or until
golden brown.

Leave to cool on a wire rack. Meanwhile, put the
chocolate pieces in a heatproof bowl set over a
saucepan of gently simmering water and heat until
melted. Stir the chocolate, then leave to cool
slightly. Use a spoon to drizzle the chocolate in
waves over the biscuits, or spoon into a piping
bag and pipe zig-zag lines over the biscuits. Chill
in an airtight container in the refrigerator for
30 minutes before serving.

makes 30 | prep 15 mins, plus 30 mins' chilling | cook 15 mins

chocolate & brazil nut crunchies

INGREDIENTS

55 g/2 oz butter or margarine, plus extra
  for greasing
55 g/2 oz white vegetable fat
140 g/5 oz demerara sugar
1 egg
1 tsp vanilla essence
1 tbsp milk
100 g/3½ oz plain flour, unsifted
100 g/3½ oz rolled oats
1 tsp bicarbonate of soda
pinch of salt
175 g/6 oz plain chocolate chips
75 g/2¼ oz Brazil nuts, chopped

Put the butter, fat, sugar, egg, vanilla essence and milk in a blender or food processor and process for at least 3 minutes until a fluffy consistency is reached.

Mix the flour, oats, bicarbonate of soda and salt together in a large bowl. Stir in the egg mixture, then the chocolate chips and nuts and mix well together. Cover the bowl with clingfilm and chill in the refrigerator for 30 minutes until firm.

Meanwhile, preheat the oven to 180°C/350°F/Gas Mark 4. Grease a large baking tray.

Put 30 rounded tablespoonfuls of the mixture onto the prepared baking tray, making sure that they are well spaced. Bake in the preheated oven for 15 minutes, or until golden brown.

Leave to cool on a wire rack before serving.

Index